Dynamics of Spiritual Growth & Maturity

Dynamics of Spiritual Growth & Maturity

E. C. Nakeli

King's Word Publishing

© 2018 by E.C. Nakeli

Published by King's Word Publication

For your questions and publishing needs, write to:

    CMFI
    40 S Church st
    Westminster, MD 21157
    E-mail: *ecnakeli@yahoo.com*

Printed in the United States of America

All rights reserved. No part of this publication may be reproduced, stored in a retrieval systems, or transmitted in ay form or by any means— for example, electronic, photocopy, recording—without the prior written permission of the publisher. The only exception is brief quotations in printed reviews.

E.C. Nakeli

To contact the author, write to:

    E.C. Nakeli
    40 S Church st
    Westminster, MD 21157
    E-mail: *ecnakeli@yahoo.com*

Dynamics of Spiritual Growth and Maturity/
E.C. Nakeli

ISBN: 97819450551881

    Unless otherwise indicated, Scriptures references are from
    THE HOLY BIBLE, NEW INTERNATIONAL VERSION®, NIV®
    Copyright © 1973, 1978, 1984, 2011 by Biblica, Inc™
    Used by permission. All rights reserved worlwide.

Cover and interior design by Zach Essama

Photo cover: iStockphoto.com | Photo ID:471158558 | with authorization

Table of Contents

Introduction 1

Part One

Chapter 1: Your growth is reflected in,
and determined by giving 5

Chapter 2: Your growth is reflected in,
and determined by reading (research) 21

Chapter 3: Your growth is determined by,
and reflected in obedience 27

Chapter 4: Your growth is determined by,
and reflected in worship 35

Chapter 5: Your growth is determined by,
and reflected in trustworthiness 45

Chapter 6: Your growth is determined by,
and reflected in humility 49

Part Two

Chapter 7: Maturity 61

Chapter 8: Your degree of maturity is determined by,
and reflected in, your meditations 73

Chapter 9: Your maturity is determined by,
and reflected in your attitude 79

Chapter 10: Your maturity is determined by,
and reflected in, your teachability 87

Chapter 11: Your maturity is determined by,
and reflected in, your understanding 93

Chapter 12: Your maturity is determined by,
and reflected in, your responsibility 97
Chapter 13: Your maturity is determined by,
and reflected in, your initiative 109
Chapter14: Your maturity is determined by,
and reflected in, your capacity to trust..115
Chapter 15: Your maturity is determined by,
and reflected in, your capacity to yield..127

Conclusion.. **133**

INTRODUCTION

In this study, we are going to examine growth and maturity in the light of the word of God. We are going to use the initial of each word above to see how we can measure and enhance our level of growth, how we can grow and mature in the things of God and demonstrate the power we have in Christ Jesus. I do not write as one who has arrived in all these areas but as one who has seen the need and the possibility to stretch, with our God–given elasticity, to a supernatural length, height, breadth and depth.

Part One

CHAPTER 1

YOUR GROWTH IS REFLECTED IN, AND DETERMINED BY GIVING

We all know that when a baby is born, all it does is to receive everything from its mother. As it becomes a toddler it seeks to possess everything around it, grabbing from left and right, front and back, irrespective of who owns what. As it grows further it becomes interested in the welfare of others and it may even begin to share with others what has been given it.

This is also true in the spiritual. Babies always want to receive and hardly offer anything to anybody. They are always on the receiving end as far as visits, ministry, encouragement, prayers, help, etc. are concerned. Babies always want attention and scarcely give others the attention they may need. Have you ever attempted to get the attention of a child caught up in its world, how did it look like? That is just how spiritual babies are. They are not interested in the welfare of anybody; at best they can be for a few close friends who are also interested in them. Some children grow past this stage very quickly in life, meanwhile some 'adults' have never past the childhood stage though they may appear fully grown. When you weigh the real man in them, you find them wanting in many ways.

Giving to others is one way of measuring how grown up a person is. It can mean giving oneself or one's goods. Although it is easier to give away your goods without actually giving yourself to someone, there is greater impact when the whole man is involved. This is seen in the supreme example of our Lord Jesus Christ who gave everything including Himself in the salvation package.

Now before we go any further I will like you to answer the following questions:
- When is the last time you made a gift to God?
- When is the last time you gave to somebody?
- When is the last time you made a gift to someone who merits nothing from you?
- It may have been a smile, a smile, a word of encouragement, a little gift, some money, food to the hungry, clothes to the naked etc.

Your growth is reflected in the quality of what you give to God

God looks at the quality of your gift! You know what Jesus said about the widow's mite? It was just a mite, but it was all she had. It is not what is given that qualifies the gift but what is kept for one's self. Those who only give out of abundance have not grown, just like a child will only give what it cannot consume. The mature give even out of the little they have.

Some people give only tithes, because the bible demands it, and may be with a little dime on the tithes, to represent an offering. This is just a sign of spiritual babyhood, not going beyond the minimum requirement. The one who has grown has also learnt to give and seeks to give more than what is required. It becomes a matter of a heart that overflows with love to the objects of its love. It talks of a heart that has grown to enjoy some intimacy with the object of its love.

Are you still giving as you did when you just believed, or have you made progress in the quality of your gift? In the domain of giving, are you still where you were a few years ago? Professor Fomum said money is directional, i.e. a man's money increasingly flows towards where his heart is going and vice versa.

Your growth is also reflected in how much you give to others

I am not talking here of giving to those who are your immediate responsibility but to those to whom you have no legal obligations.

Children give only to those they know and whom they know seek their interest. The mature give even to those they do not know, even those who may seemingly be their enemies. They have learnt to look beyond themselves to behold the needs of others. Mature hearts are filled with compassion for others; they look at the need and not the one who has it. For many of us the problem is that we often see the one in need other than the need and our prejudices often block the flow of compassion.

Let us look at what Scripture has to say about this:

"Out of the most severe trial, their overflowing joy and their extreme poverty welled up in rich generosity. For I testify that they gave as much as they were able, and even beyond their ability. Entirely on their own, they urgently pleaded with us for the privilege of sharing in this service to the saints. And they did not do as we expected, but they gave themselves first to the Lord and then to us in keeping with God's will." (2 Corinthians 8:2-4)

Here Paul is talking about the Macedonian churches. He says the gift they made was not out of overflowing abundance but out of:

1. Most severe trial
2. Overflowing joy
3. Extreme poverty.

Do not give only when all the circumstances around you are very favourable, if you do you will never make any gift of consequence. Your most trying moment is the best moment you can make the best gift to the worst person. That is a sign of true maturity. Just look at the words qualifying the state of those Macedonians; most severe, extreme. Surely, they had learnt to count it all joy when they passed through trials as James recommended to us. If we also count it all joy in any situation then others will begin benefiting. The Macedonians did not only give out of their poverty, but they gave beyond what they were able to give. They got into the realm of giving according to the resources heaven had placed at their disposal. This is the secret of mature giving; tapping from the heavenly resources.

Secondly, they saw it a privilege to give, not a duty. The mature give out of joy and count it a privilege to be able to give. Children see it as a duty and though they may give, they will do so grudgingly. You know Moses instructed the Israelites on how to treat the poor: *"Give generously to him and do so without a grudging heart; then because of this the LORD your God will bless you in all your work and in everything you put your hand to. There will always be a poor people in the land. Therefore, I command you to be openhanded toward your brothers and toward the poor and the needy in your land."* (Deuteronomy 15:10-11)

When you give, let it be with a joyful heart and not with a grudging heart. A grudging heart will nullify the effects of your gift and deprive you of the rewards. Another thing we can learn from these Macedonians is that the secret of joyful giving is to give oneself to the Lord first. Attempting to give joyfully and effectively without first giving oneself to the Lord can be very frustrating. There is no way you can give to God's work and to others and derive true joy from the act without a total and unreserved giving of yourself to the Lord. Your life must have been laid down once and for all at His feet in order for you to enjoy the joy of giving.

Give from your heart

"Remember this: Whoever sows sparingly will reap sparingly, and whoever sows generously will also reap generously. Each man should give what he has decided in his heart to give, not reluctantly or under compulsion, for God loves a cheerful giver. And God is able to make all grace abound to you, so that in all things at all times, having all that you need, you will abound in every good work (…) Now he who supplies seed to the sower and bread for food will also supply and increase your store of seed and will enlarge the harvest of your righteousness. You will be made rich in every way so that you can be generous in every occasion, and through us your generosity will result in thanksgiving to God." (2 Corinthians 9:6-8, 9-10).

From the above passage we can bring out the following qualities of mature giving:

1. Give generously
2. Give decidedly
3. Give cheerfully

Verse nine of the passage above talks of seed to the sower and bread for food. For everything we receive from the Lord, we must be able to distinguish which portion is seed for us to sow in the work of God and the lives of others, and which is bread for our food. The problem with many of us is that we seem to be converting seed into bread for our food and so during harvest season we do not reap anything because the seed we were supposed to sow was turned to bread for food. Likewise, at times we do not reap because what we sowed was not seed but bread that was supposed to be eaten.

The mature do not give on impulse; they give according to the need and the validation from the inward witness. You know there are people who want to give to everything. Their purpose is to obtain the applause of men so much so that what was meant to be bread is used as seed. Their children's bread is sown into fallow ground and at harvest time they have nothing to show. These are the people who then become mockers of the seed-faith teaching. They did not discern what to give and when to give and to who to give.

Before you give ensure that the Holy Spirit is validating that gift. He is the only One who can tell you whether the seed sown will yield a harvest or not.

Poverty: a blessing or a curse?

There is one passage in the Book, which I do love very much because it treats on the practical aspects of giving. Let us quote part of the passage and we shall concentrate on the verses which deal with our subject at hand.

> "However, there should be no poor among you, for in the land the
> LORD your God is giving you to possess as your inheritance, he will
> richly bless you, if only you fully obey the LORD your God and are

careful to follow all these commands I am giving you today. For the LORD your God will bless you as he has promised, and you will lend to many nations but will borrow from none. You will rule over many nations, but none will rule over you.

If there is a poor man among your brothers in any of the towns of the land that the LORD your God is giving you, do not be hardhearted or tightfisted toward your poor brother. Rather be openhanded and freely lend him whatever he needs. Be careful not to harbor this wicked thought: "The seventh year, the year for canceling debts, is near," so that you do not show ill will toward your needy brother and give him nothing. He may then appeal to the LORD against you, and you will be found guilty of sin. Give generously to him and do so without a grudging heart; then because of this the LORD your God will bless you in all your work and in everything you put your hand to. There will always be poor people in the land. Therefore, I command you to be openhanded toward your brothers and toward the poor and needy in your land." (Deuteronomy 15:4-11)

Poverty is not God's will for you or for anyone of His covenant people. God has richly filled your days with His abundance. Verse four of our passage says, there should be no poor among God's children. God has richly blessed each one of us. That is why the apostle Paul, by the Holy Spirit could say, *"Praise be to the God and Father of our LORD Jesus Christ, who has blessed us in the heavenly realms with every spiritual blessing in Christ."* (Ephesians 1:3). He has blessed us and has shown us the way to tap the blessings and bring them down to our realm. Let me reiterate that poverty among God's covenant people is a curse. It should not exist at all. I am not talking of sacrificial living for the sake of the cross but the kind of life in which we cannot meet our most basic needs and even give to others or the work of God.

It is possible for there to be no poor or any trace of poverty among God's covenant people. The abnormality is that *"If there is a poor man among you…"* God knows that some amongst His covenant people will fail to tap from the abundance He has for them. And so, He commands us not to be hard-hearted or tight-fisted towards that individual.

Hard-heartedness and tightfistedness go hand in glove. The condition of your heart towards someone or something determines the reaction of your fist towards that individual. Hard-heartedness talks of refusing to feel for someone. It talks of refusing to be moved towards that individual, with compassion.

It is talks of holding back what should normally flow to others. Hard-heartedness can never go with open-handedness. Likewise, a soft-hearted man will always be an open-handed man. The Lord commands us to tap from His infinite reservoir of blessings by freely giving to others what they need, and we are able to provide. To give freely means to give with no strings attached. Not even an expectation of a *"thank you"* should be attached to our acts of kindness.

A way of life

>Verse eight says, *"Rather be…"*
>*God does not look at your occasional acts of goodness, but He wants you to be open-handed. He wants it to be your way of life.*
>*An open hand does not withhold anything.*
>*An open hand has no grip on anything*
>*An open hand passes on what it receives*
>*An open hand lets go what has to go*
>*An open hand results from a soft heart*

Growth is reflected in and determined by open-handedness. The more open-handed you are, the more you grow in all domains of life. The more mature you are the more open-handed you are.

>*"… and freely lend him whatever he needs…"*

There should be no constraint in giving to those in need. There should be no preconditions. Your responsibility is to give without interruption; un-reluctantly and unreservedly. Now, if God wants you to meet any need, then He must have blessed you with all it takes to meet it irrespective of its magnitude. He uses any means no matter how small or big, no matter how important or unimportant it maybe. God's will for you is that you are in such a position to identify needs and freely meet them. Verse nine of our passage says when we fail to meet the needs of those we are well able to help, God will count it as a sin against us. When you fail to meet the need of a brother or sister when in a position to do so, even for the most genuine reason, you sin.

The main reason why men are stingy is that they think about their own needs. As long as your mind is occupied with your own needs, it is practically impossible to meet the needs of another, even if they are more pressing. That is why the Lord Jesus said, *"Do not think about these things"* (Luke12:29) – personal needs. As long as you can identify the need of a fellow believer and you are in a position to help, go ahead and meet that need. Do not wait for some special leading from the Lord. God will only lead you to meet needs which are not evident. It is your responsibility to meet those needs which are already known to you.

An open door

Now the secret to growth (whether social, material, financial or spiritual) is giving.

> *"Give generously to those in need around you, then*
> 1. Your God will bless you in all your work
> 2. Your God will bless you in everything you put your hand to.

That is the open door into the blessed life. You see many people make gifts but most often they make gifts to those who do not need the things or who can afford those things. God says we should be generous towards the poor of the land and not the rich. The corrupt nature of our society has made it such that even the poor will want to offer gifts to the rich. But this is what the Word says, *"There will always be poor people in the land. Therefore I command you to be openhanded toward your brothers and toward the poor and needy in your land"* (Deuteronomy 15:11).

There will always be people whose need you can meet. There will always be people whom you are more privileged than materially or financially. Make it a life style to be a blessing to the less privileged around you. There is at least one person you can help. There will always be an opportunity for you to provoke God's blessings through acts of generosity.

Open-handedness is a command and not an option. To be tight-fisted is a sin because it is clear-cut disobedience to a command. Your open-handedness must be

1. Towards your brethren
2. Towards the poor and needy in the land.

That is, God expects you to meet primarily the needs of those in the church (Galatians 6:10) but also that you go beyond the confines of the church to meeting even the needs of the unsaved. Your generosity should begin with but must not be limited to those in the church. Verse fourteen gives us another startling truth: *"Supply him liberally from your flock, your threshing floor and your winepress. Give to him as the LORD your God has blessed you"*.

Giving is a proclamation of how far you believe God has blessed you. The degree of your gratitude is reflected in giving.

- Failure to give is proclaiming that God has not blessed you.
- Giving a little is proclaiming that God has blessed you just a little.
- Giving much is proclaiming that God has blessed you much.
- Reducing your giving is proclaiming that God has withdrawn some of His blessings
- Maintain a certain constant giving is proclaiming that you are not growing in blessing.

Giving, both to God and to the needy, is either true or false depending on whether it is a true reflection of how God has blessed you or not. To give less than what you ought to is to ask God to reduce your blessing. To give more than you are supposed to is to ask God to increase your blessing and take you to a new level. Giving is prophetic; blessings respond to giving. Giving to others and to God determines how much you will receive from others and from God.

> *"Each of you must bring a gift in proportion to the way the LORD your God has blessed you"* (Deuteronomy 16:17).

You are expected to give in proportion to what God has blessed you. He does not expect you to give in a smaller proportion to what He has blessed you. He does not expect you to give, as a way of life, greater than the proportion to which He has blessed you. Giving beyond your ability is not the normal but the occasional.

Occasionally you can stretch yourself financially but let it not be the norm that will negatively affect those who depend directly on you. You can decide to live in poverty because you want to give to others and to God's work, but your consecration should not be imposed on those for whose needs you are directly responsible. They are your primary responsibility before anything else.

God Wants you to Abound

> *"Remember this: Whoever sows sparingly will also reap sparingly, and whoever sows generously will also reap generously. Each man should give what he has decided in his heart to give, not reluctantly or under compulsion, for God loves a cheerful giver. And God is able to make all grace abound to you, so that in all things at all times, having all that you need, you will abound in every good work. As it is written:*
> *'He has scattered abroad his gifts to the poor;*
> *his righteousness endures forever.'*
> *Now he who supplies seed to the sower and bread for food will also supply and increase your store of seed and will enlarge the harvest of your righteousness. You will be made rich in every way so that you can be generous on every occasion, and through us your generosity will result in thanksgiving to God."* (2 Corinthians 9:6-11)

One of the principles of life is that you will reap what you sow in the same proportion, no matter who you are and what you sow. Generosity is an avenue for growth in every area of a man's life.

God cannot and does not compel you to give (except for tithes and offerings which are a must) but wants you to decide in your own heart what to give. God's will is that you give out of a heart that overflows. If you base your giving on calculation you will obviously make no progress in your spiritual life.

God's arithmetic does not follow our human logic and so bringing it will block our blessing. Give not what you have decided in your head or your mind or your emotions but what you have decided in your heart (spirit). For it to bear fruits, the decision must be that of the spirit. When the decision to give springs from your spirit, giving becomes a cheerful exercise and the blessings and reaped. When this happens, you can then expect the following blessings:

1. A revelation of God's ability:

"And God..."

This is the God who created the whole universe, the One who possesses everything visible and invisible. We are talking of the God who brings into existence things which are not and takes out of existence things which are. He is the One to whom belong all the gold and silver in heaven and on earth, the One who owns the cattle on a thousand hills.

"And God is..."

He is not a God of yesterday or of times past. He is a God of today too. He is a God of tomorrow. He spans eternity. He is Jesus Christ the same yesterday, today and forever. He is up to date. He revealed Himself to Moses as the *"I AM that I AM"*. God wants to be current in your life. Cheerful giving is just one of those ways which will cause Him to reveal Himself to you in your current situation. How He longs to make Himself real to you. Giving opens the door for him to come in and manifest His ability in you and through you.

"And God is able..."

The extent to which you sow or give generously is the extent to which God will demonstrate His infinite super abilities in your life and through you. When we talk of giving here we do not limit ourselves to finances. There is a lot more to give than just money.

You can give your love…
You can give encouragement
You can give hospitality
You can give your wisdom
You can give counsel
… and many more things!

2. Your life will be full of grace.

"And God is able to make all grace abound to you…"

In other words God wants to fill your life with Divine enabling. When God's grace is in all you do, you will have a super blessed life. You receive insight where others are dumbfounded. You accomplish in one day what others accomplish in a week.

Your whole life will abound with grace!
Grace to remain healthy!
Grace to remain strong!
Grace to make spiritual progress!
Grace to live holy!
Grace to love everybody!
Grace to be at peace with all men!
Grace to live with the most difficult person in the most difficult circumstance!
Grace to receive revelations!
Grace to have a following!
Grace to do all you have been called to do!

God wants to fill you with the divine ability to function. That is grace! That grace is so that in all things – great things, small things, things in the limelight, things in secret; seemingly insignificant things and things that can be acclaimed; you can excel and be the best. That grace is in all things at all times. All times – in the morning, at noon, in the evening, at night! When you are asleep or when you are awake. Life is completely different and better when you can tap from God's grace at will.

3. You will be sufficiently supplied

"Having all you need…"

God wants us to live permanently in a place where all of our needs are met–material, physical, emotional, moral, mental, financial, social or spiritual needs. He wants you to *"have all you need…"*

O! There is a place where all our needs can be met. We were not meant to be lopsided. God wants us to be wholly balanced. There are some people who abound financially but are social misfits. Others abound materially and socially but not as far as the moral and spiritual aspects of life are concerned.

God wants you to grow proportionately in all domains so that you will be wholesome and balanced. Many of us rejoice when some of our needs are met. Some think it is heaven on earth when most of their needs are met. God wants to give us more, not just some of our needs, not even most of our needs but all of our needs. O, God take me to this level. I am not yet there, I seem to have visited it for a season but now I want to make it my permanent dwelling place. My Father help me explore this avenue of giving which leads to such a life.

When the apostle Paul wrote *"And my God will meet all your needs according to His glorious riches in Christ Jesus"* (Philippians 4:19), he meant it. He spoke by the spirit of the Living God. The word of God is true. If you believe it an act on it you shall reap the fruits of that life of obedient faith.

"Having all you need…" May we all get to that level. Some people are already there and are enjoying that blessed life. However, it is not a place for a few. There can never be overcrowding there. He has made enough room for each one of us to accommodate those who are in the street called "Having all you need". It is not a place for a privileged few.

4. "You will be made rich…"

This portrays you as passive. God's work in you makes you rich. That is why the Lord of all glory said *"all these things will be added to you"*. Who does the addition? God of course! You cannot make yourself wholly rich, only God can do that. He does that by

a. **Making all grace abound to you (v 8)**
   - Grace to make the right choices
   - Grace to make the right decisions
   - Grace to be looked upon with favour
   - Grace to build the right relationships
   - Grace to conceive the right ideas
   - Grace to make the right investments

b. **Increasing your store of seeds (v 10)**

   This is enlarging your capacity to sow in the lives and ministries of others. This is so that you can sow in the kingdom business and thereby reap the fruits thereof. Seed is meant to be sowed. Unfortunately many of us, instead of sowing the increased store of seeds God has given us, convert it to *"bread"*. Seed is for sowing! If you sow the right seeds in the right reason, you will surely reap your harvest of a hundred or sixty or thirty folds

c. **Increasing the harvest of your righteousness (v 10)**

   This means God will multiply the yield of all that you do for righteousness sake.

d. **Giving you the ability (skill, talent, ideas)**

   To make wealth: *"But remember the LORD your God, for it is he who gives you the ability to produce wealth, and so confirms his covenant, which he swore to your forefathers, as it is today"* Deuteronomy 8:18).

   God will make you rich by giving you the ability to make wealth. He will lead you to make the right investments. He will lead you to do the right business in the right seasons.

e. You will concerned by the welfare of others

"… so that you can be generous on every occasion…"

There is a good reason, an overriding purpose why God makes you rich. Making you rich is not the end point but a means to a greater objective God wants to accomplish through you. God wants to make you rich so that He can reach out to the less privilege through you. The conjunctive phrase *"so that"* tells you that being made rich is not all about you, but about others.

The next phrase *"you can"* has to do with the power, potential, ability, or capability to do something. It means to be in a disposition, ready to do something.

"Can" is to be able to flow freely, with some mastery of what you do. God is making you rich so that you will be ready to help those in need.

Take a look now at the next phrase *"Be generous…"*

The Father will make you rich so that generosity will become a part and parcel of your life. Generosity must not be foreign to any child of God; it must be built in the very fabric of your being. God does not only want you to practice generosity. He wants it to be your nature. To be generous means to be kind hearted, to freely give to those who are in need. It means to joyfully meet the needs of those you have no obligation to. God wants you to be generous on every occasion. This means irrespective of the person in need, irrespective of where or what the need is.

You can become financially rich!
You can become materially rich!
You can become rich in mercy!
You can become rich in love!
You can become rich in service!
You can become rich in encouraging others!

God has shown you the way. It is your responsibility to walk through that path.

CHAPTER 2

YOUR GROWTH IS REFLECTED IN, AND DETERMINED BY READING (Research)

Progress in any area of life is tied to discovery. And discovery is the product of research. Growth to spiritual maturity is also enhanced by discovery. It is a function of revelation and revelation comes through research. Spiritual research is carried out in God's word, as you read and meditate on it profoundly. When you expose yourself to the word of God the Holy Spirit – the Revealer of God's mysteries – illuminates your mind on certain issues and grants you spiritual knowledge. Your degree of spiritual knowledge determines growth in depth, height, weight and girth. The Lord commands us to *"Look in the scroll of the LORD and read"* (Isaiah 34:16a). When you look in, it teaches you and supplies your spirit with necessary nutrients for growth.

Bishop Oyedepo wrote:

"Life that is void of progress is a burden. Stagnation is the mother of frustration. There is need to apply yourself to the vital forces that ensure increase in the anointing. And you are the one to make it happen, as it never happens on its own. The key factor for growth in the anointing is the word of God." He further writes

"Meditation in the word is the principal way to keep your mind healthy, active, resourceful and productive. Qualitative meditation (not just reading, but pondering on the Word in your mind), is rubbing your little mind with the great mind of the creator.

And because iron sharpens iron, the creator's great mind begins to sharpen your little mind, upgrading and increasing its capacity to function." (David O. Oyedepo, *Understanding the Anointing*, Dominion Publishing House)

Rev. Kenneth E. Hagin said he read the New Testament over a hundred and fifty times before he started preaching. He linked his growth in ministry to the effect of God's word in his life. Another great man of God Smith Wigglesworth said he often placed a price for anyone who will succeed to catch him anywhere without his Bible. He ensured that he read it often. Professor Zach Fomum said he owes his success in ministry to his life of meditation on the Word of God.

There is no greater secret to spiritual growth and maturity like spending time in God's word, reading widely and reading profoundly (meditation).

It is written; *"For Ezra had devoted himself to the study and observance of the Laws of the LORD, and to teaching its decrees and laws in Israel."* (Ezra 7:10).

Here we see that Ezra's growth was tied to his devotion to the word of God. He was not born with the knowledge of God. He only grew in that knowledge as he read and studied. You too can rise to any height and reach any depth of the mysteries of God as you give yourself to studying it. As you study you receive spiritual knowledge. Spiritual knowledge enhances obedience which leads to growth.

"This Ezra came up from Babylon. He was a teacher well versed in the Law of Moses, which the LORD, the God of Israel, had given. The king had granted him everything he asked, for the hand of the LORD his God was on him… This is a copy of the letter King Artaxerxes had given to Ezra the priest and teacher, a man learned in matters concerning the commands and decrees of the LORD for Israel" (Ezra 7:6,11)

Ezra was versed with matters of the Law not because he was a priest or because he was *"chosen"* but he devoted himself to the word. You become an expert in anything to which you devote yourself. To grow in your knowledge of Divine ways and principles you must give yourself to fervent and diligent searching of the Book. It entails making notes and carrying out research on specific topics in the Bible. You can also study the life different Bible characters. The truth is that Christianity is all about devotion to God through His eternal word.

Are you devoted to studying the word? How much time do you put in not just to read but to systematically study God's word, laboring to get its deeper meaning? If you are to be devoted to the word then it must consume a significant part of your time, energy, finance etc. The word must become your priority if you have to grow in service in the kingdom and in your knowledge of the King.

The Bible does not say Ezra studied or read the word occasionally or as he was led. Some people are deceived to think that, they will be led to read or to study the word. You have to decide and devote yourself to it. Devotion talks of applying attention, time and oneself completely to some activity or purpose. This is exactly what Ezra did. It is said that most of the Old Testament was compiled by Ezra.

What about Solomon who was endowed with super natural wisdom? He said of himself, *"I devote myself to study and to explore by wisdom all that is done under heaven"* (Ecclesiastes 13a). You see the phrase *"devoted to study"* appearing again. My dear friend, your growth will be determined by reading or research. The more time you give to reading and research the more you grow.

Reigning with the word

God's instructions to the king of Israel was that; *"When he takes the throne of his kingdom, he is to write for himself on a scroll a copy of this law, taken from that of the priests, who are Levites. It is to be with him, and he is to read it all the days of his life so that he may learn to revere the LORD his God and follow carefully all the words of this law and these decrees"* (Deuteronomy 17:18-19).

Now the Bible also says we are a kingdom of priests. For you and me to reign on the throne on which our Lord Jesus has placed us we must heed the above instructions. The secret is reading the word daily. Do you want to reign over the kingdom of darkness and life's circumstances? Then devote yourself to the word of God.

To the young Pastor Timothy, Paul said, *"study to show thyself approved unto God, a workman that need not to be ashamed, rightly dividing the word of truth."* (2 Timothy 2:15, KJV)

For you to gain access into the mysteries of the word so as to rightly divide it, you must study. That is the simple secret.

You Can Avoid Confusion

"Search the scriptures…" (John 5:39a KJV)

You have to search the scriptures and allow the Holy Spirit to guide you therein. As you study, compare what you receive with what others have said about the passage. This will keep you under authority and protect you from the devil's deception.

A few days ago, a young man asked me a question about something he followed in a VCD. He seemed very confused. I gave him my opinion about the issue he presented and told him the view of two outstanding men of God; that brought him relief as it tied with what he received when he himself searched the scriptures. Beware of teachers who claim to receive unique revelations that contradict what other authorities have taught over the years; especially when your own spirit does not bear witness to their veracity.

> It is written *"Now the Bereans were of more noble character than the Thessalonians, for they received the message with great eagerness and examined the Scriptures every day to see if what Paul said was true. Many of the Jews believed, as did also a number of prominent Greek women and many Greek men"* (Acts 17:11-12).

After listening to the word taught by somebody, instead of getting confused or taking offence, sit down and examine the scriptures to receive approval or disapproval of what you have heard. Reading and research will determine your growth. You should read what others have written on different subjects pertaining to the Christian life. This will teach you many things and encourage you in your private study. You know as I have meditated on the word and written down what I received, in reading Christian literature I am very encouraged to discover that the Holy Spirit can reveal to me what He reveals to great men of God. He can teach me what He has taught others. Books written by anointed men of God widen your scope and expand your horizon. Some will correct you where you are wrong.

Just as reading and research determine your growth, the latter is reflected in your reading and research. You can assess someone's level of spiritual maturity through the persons reading, studying and meditating on the word of God. Some years ago Dr. Myles Munroe said he reads a new book every week and one magazine every week. This is a sign of maturity. You know you have to compel a child to study. After an effort he or she will study against his or her will. But as one matures he or she takes the initiative to study. In fact as you climb the academic ladder you seek avenues for scholarship. You make proposals on new areas of research. It is the same thing in the Christian life. As you grow spiritually, you take the initiative to study the word of God. You give more time to study the word and to find out what others have said on certain issues.

CHAPTER 3

YOUR GROWTH IS DETERMINED BY, AND REFLECTED IN OBEDIENCE

Another determinant factor, in fact the most determinant, of growth is obedience. Reading and research lead to revelation which brings you to the point of obedience. The one to whom little has been revealed and who obeys the little will grow faster and more steadily than he to whom much has been revealed but who has not obeyed. In fact, the only purpose of spiritual knowledge i.e. the only purpose of revelation is to enhance obedience.

The Bible says *"The secret things belong to the LORD our God, but the things revealed belong to us and to our children forever that we may follow all the words of this law."* (Deuteronomy 29:29). The things revealed are for you to obey, to model your life according to what is written. If all your reading and research is only for mere carnal knowledge then you have missed it all. Reading and research are good but it does not end there. Until you have modeled your life according to your discoveries then one who never read or researched is far better than you are.

Again it is written; *"For Ezra had devoted himself to the study and observance of the law of the LORD, and to teaching its decrees and laws in Israel."* (Ezra 7:10).

I want you to take note of the sequence
1. He devoted himself to study of the law
2. He devoted himself to observance of the law
3. He devoted himself to teaching of the law.

Observance of the law refers to obeying the Word. It talks of living according to the Word and applying what you have studied to your own life. It talks of living the practicalities of God's word. The Word is not observed by mere desire or wish but by a deliberate act of devotion to the observance of every aspect of it. If you are a Bible teacher, your teaching will have little or no impact until you observe what you teach. Study without observance is mere form without any value. In fact it only retards the growth of the one who studies but does not obey or apply the knowledge received. Unless obedience to the word becomes an integral must of your life you cannot make any progress.

The Bedrock Of Growth

> *"But Samuel replied: "Does the LORD delight in burnt offerings and sacrifices as much as in obeying the voice of the LORD? To obey is better than sacrifice, and to heed is better than the fat of rams." (1 Samuel 15:22)*

Every other factor of growth depends largely on this one factor – obedience. If you take obedience out of your life, though all the other factors may be in place; growth becomes impossibility. Remember we said sacrificial giving also enhances growth in the kingdom. However God lets us to know that sacrifice plus disobedience equals rebellion. You cannot give to God or to His people in disobedience.

You cannot read and research, and receive revelations while living in disobedience. You cannot worship while living in disobedience. When you cease to obey you cease to grow. In fact you begin to retrogress. There is no stagnancy in the Christian life; it is either a forward motion or a backward motion. You are either ascending or you are descending. The Lord told the Israelites,

> *"For when I brought your forefathers out of Egypt and spoke to them, I did not just give them commands about burnt offerings and sacrifices, but I gave them this command: Obey me, and I will be your*

> *God and you will be my people. Walk in all the ways I command you that it may go well with you. But they did not listen or pay attention; instead, they followed the stubborn inclinations of their evil hearts. They went backward and not forward"* (Jeremiah 7:22-24).

You see, like many today, the Israelites had become interested only in the sacrifices instead of obedience. Your well being in every aspect of your life lies only in your capacity to obey.

Most often God's commands conflict with your own set ways and principles. They also conflict human traditions as well as the *"ethics"* of some societies, cultures and profession. In such situations all you have to do is to obey the word of God. This is what we learn from the apostles throughout the book of Acts. There is no excuse to disobey God and obey the ethics of your culture and profession. Remember Solomon, speaking by the spirit of God said, *"Fear God and keep his commandments, for this is the whole (duty) of man"* (Ecclesiastes 12:13b).

You can ask the Holy Spirit to show you areas where you might be ignorantly living in disobedience. If you know any area you had better put things in order so that other things will begin holding together.

The Price Of Success

> *"Do not let this Book of the Law depart from your mouth; meditate on it day and night, so that you may be careful to do everything written in it. Then you will be prosperous and successful."*
> (Josuah 1:8)

The price of success is obedience to the Word. God told Joshua not to allow the Book to depart from his mouth. This means the Book will attempt to depart from his mouth and so he needed to exercise some personal discipline to ensure that it does not depart. Those who think that their attitude towards the word will always naturally favor their attention are in for a great shock. Almost everything around you will attempt to hinder you from giving the needed attention to God's

Word. If you keep this in mind then you will be quick to recognize the subtle oppositions from the enemy.

The Lord is pointing out that the price of lasting success and prosperity lies in constant meditation on the word. As you meditate on the Word, your spirit is fortified and enabled to render wholehearted obedience to God. Meditation on God's word stimulates complete obedience to the eternal word of God.

Also meditation gives the Holy Spirit the opportunity to point out anything in the heart of a man which may hinder growth. You know sin and other acts of disobedience are like parasites which hinder the growth of their host. They feed on the best of the nutrients and leave you with what cannot truly sustain.

Those who give the needed attention to the word of God find it very easy to obey. Why? Because exposure, I mean constant and continuous exposure, to the word gives the Holy Spirit the opportunity to make the will become flexible, malleable and ductile in the hands of the living God. Man is naturally stubborn and prone to the stubborn inclinations of his heart. And this only makes him to regress instead of progressing and prospering in the true sense of it. You want to succeed? Obedience is the price! Meditation on God's word enhances obedience.

The Key To Spiritual Knowledge

> *"If any of you really determines to do God's will, then you will certainly know whether my teaching is from God or is merely my own"* (John 7:17 Living Bible).

> *"To the Jews who had believed him, Jesus said, "If you hold to my teaching, you are really my disciples. Then you will know the truth, and the truth will set you free"* (John 8:31-32).

The key to growth is revelation knowledge, when the spirit receives and conveys to the natural man, insight from the Holy Spirit. At such a time, a man knows that he knows a thing. Spiritual knowledge enhances growth and maturity in the Christian life.

If the key to growth is spiritual knowledge, then what is the key to spiritual knowledge? Obedience is the key! Obedience to God's word is a matter of choice. The NIV renders John 7:17 as, *"If a man chooses to do God's will…"* If you have to obey God, you must choose to do so, you must make up your mind i.e. be determined to. This is the key of revelations or spiritual knowledge. God reveals the mysteries and give the parts of the kingdom to those who are disposed to obey. Once your heart is inclined towards obedient action, you have cheap access to the mysteries of the kingdom.

Jesus said when a man continues in, holds to, lives according to His teachings, he will know the truth. And that knowledge sets free from the captivity and bondage which results from ignorance. Ignorance is a cruel captor which seldom wants to let go its captives until it is compelled to. What compels it to let go its captivities is what we call spiritual knowledge whose entrance key is obedience to God's word.

Your Entrance Key

In Luke 8:21 the Lord Jesus Christ points out that the entrance key to a living and personal relationship with Him is obedience to the word of God. For you to maintain a vibrant and consequential relationship with the Master, you have to listen to the word of God and keep it.

> *"My mother and brothers are those who hear God's word and put it into practice"* (Luke 8:21).

Obedience – the practice of God's word – brings you into a filial relationship with the Master. He does not only want to be your Lord and Savior but He wants to be known to you as a brother. Isn't it great to be the brother of the Great King?

> It will also be your entrance key into the kingdom of heaven.
> *"Not everyone who says to me, 'Lord, Lord,' will enter the kingdom of heaven, but only he who does the will of my Father who is in heaven"* (Matthew 7:21).

It gives you access to the power and authority of the kingdom. It gives you access to the rights and privileges of the sons of the kingdom. It also grants you access to the blessings of the kingdom (see Deuteronomy 28, Exodus 19:5, Job 36:11).

The Secret to Obedient Living

Many of us can easily obey if we understand the secret to obedience. Do you which to know the secret? It is right within your reach. It is called <u>immediate response</u>. By immediate response I mean the necessary action in response to the command or revelation in question. This has been the secret of the heroes of the kingdom. Study the life of Noah, Abraham, David, Paul and the like, you will notice that they made maximum use of the tremendous power that is released when one acts immediately on divine instructions.

> *"On that very day Abraham took his son Ishmael and all those born in his household or bought with his money, every male in his household, and circumcised them, as God told him"* (Genesis 17:23).

> *"Early the next morning Abraham took some food and a skin of water and gave them to Hagar. He set them on her shoulders and then sent her off with the boy. She went on her way and wandered in the desert of Beersheba"* (Genesis 21:14).

> *"Early the next morning Abraham got up and saddled his donkey. He took with him two of his servants and his son Isaac. When he had cut enough wood for the burnt offering, he set out for the place God had told him about"* (Genesis 22:3).

> *"After Paul had seen the vision, we got ready at once to leave for Macedonia, concluding that God had called us to preach the gospel to them"* (Acts 16:10).

In fact obedience is equivalent to walking in the light. Obedience is like a plant's response to light. Just as a plant's response to stimuli (light) determines its growth, so does your response to spiritual stimuli (light of revelation) determine growth. If you have a poor response to revelation light you will become stunted and lopsided in your spiritual build up.

There is a phrase *"healthy growth"* which means that there is a kind of growth which is not healthy. Talking about growth, we want to emphasize that you grow in a healthy manner. Obedience balances all the other factors that enhance growth and ensures that you grow in a healthy manner. Do not become a big-headed, large-bellied, tiny-legged individual. Discourage any manner of dysfunctional growth in your spiritual build up by living in obedience.

Obedience enhances fellowship with the God head and fellowship keeps you spiritually fit and healthy. Besides, the healthier a man is the more readily he obeys. You can estimate your level of spiritual growth and maturity by measuring your obedience.

How willingly do you obey?

How readily do you obey?

How *"totally and completely"* do you obey?

How *"precisely"* do you obey?

An honest response to the above questions will give you a picture of your level of maturity.

CHAPTER 4

YOUR GROWTH IS DETERMINED BY, AND REFLECTED IN WORSHIP

Your worship life determines a lot about your growth. A person with a poor worship life will be stunted and lopsided in his or her growth. In fact lack of constant and deep worship retards spiritual growth. It should be noted that when I talk of worship here I mean, worship, praise, and thanksgiving and service inclusive. The King of glory said, *"Yet a time is coming and has now come when the true worshipers will worship the Father in spirit and truth, for they are the kind of worshipers the Father seeks. God is spirit, and his worshipers must worship in spirit and in truth"* (John 4:23-24).

Worship Is A Command

> *"Worship the LORD your God, and his blessing will be on your food and water. I will take away sickness from among you, and none will miscarry or be barren in your land. I will give you a full life span. "I will send my terror ahead of you and throw into confusion every nation you encounter. I will make all your enemies turn their backs and run. I will send the hornet ahead of you to drive the Hivites, Canaanites and Hittites out of your way."*
> (Exodus 23:25-28)

"He said in a loud voice, "Fear God and give him glory, because the hour of his judgment has come. Worship him who made the heavens, the earth, the sea and the springs of water".
(Revelation 14:7)

You are commanded to the worship because worship triggers the blessings of the Most high on every aspect of one's life.

1. **It triggers growth in food supply:**
"His blessings will be on your food and water…"
This means you will have an increased supply of food and water. Drought and famine will not come near you. When what you eat and drink have God's blessing upon them they will produce the required result of physical growth.

2. **It triggers growth in health:**
"I will take away sickness from among you"
Naturally when you eat and drink healthily, you grow healthy. There are some sicknesses or crises which are a result of growth. We see this often when children are growing up. But God says even those sicknesses and crises which are tied to growth will be taken from the life of the one who worships Him.

3. **It triggers growth in numbers:**
"None will miscarry or be barren in your land".
Nothing hinders natural growth in numbers like barrenness. Someone who is barren cannot multiply himself and so he remains alone. When there are miscarriages there is no increase in numbers too. God wants to increase any community and incorporate growth in numbers. As we worship the Lord as a body the capacity to multiply ourselves will be imparted and spiritual barrenness will find no place in our midst.

4. **It triggers increase in dominion:**
"I will send my terror ahead of you and throw into confusion every nation you encounter. I will make all your enemies turn their backs and run".

This talks about exercising dominion. Worship makes you a terror to all the enemies of God's people. As you approach, they give way. In fact at your appearance they will all disperse in a confused manner. Because God's terror goes ahead of the one who worships. No enemy will be able to stand face to face with you. In fact as you grow in worship you will increasingly see the back of your enemies because they will always be on the run. God says He will drive them little by little so that you will *"increase enough to take possession of the Land"*. That is until you grow enough in strength, in numbers, in wisdom and all what it takes to possess all your possessions – all that has been allotted you in Christ.

How to Worship

If worship is to enhance growth, then we must understand how to worship because until something is done and done correctly it will not produce the required results. So if we know the results of worship we must understand how to get to the results. Telling you the effects of worship as outlined earlier on in this chapter without telling you how to worship is like telling someone of the wonders of heaven without telling the person how to get there.

1. Worship with Your Body

"Therefore, I urge you, brothers, in view of God's mercy, to offer your bodies as living sacrifices, holy and pleasing to God--this is your spiritualn act of worship" (Romans 12:1).

When you keep your body from all defilement, then you are worshipping God with it. But when you respond to the dictates of the flesh which defile the body you are worshipping the body. You have been called to *"offer your body as a living sacrifice…"* No one is allowed to offer what is defiled. God does not accept defiled food offered to Him (see Malachi, first chapter). Thus if you must offer your body as a living sacrifice it must be acceptable, that is without defilement.

So when you offer the parts of your body in service to God you are worshipping Him with your body.

2. Worship with Your Treasures

> *"On coming to the house, they saw the child with his mother Mary, and they bowed down and worshiped him. Then they opened their treasures and presented him with gifts of gold and of incense and of myrrh"* (Matthew 2:11).

Another form of worship is to worship with your treasures. These sages worshipped the new born King by pulling out their treasures and presenting them to Him. This is true worship. There is no way you can truly worship while your treasure remains in the bag. Once the body has been willingly offered to God as a sign of worship, the body will put out the treasures to enhance further worship.

What do you consider a treasure? The best thing you can do is to worship God with it by offering it to Him. Open that treasure and present Him with gifts. When you put at the service of the kingdom all that you have, you are worshipping God with your possessions and so you will not worship the possessions. Anything you cannot worship God with, you will end up worshipping. When you worship God with your treasures He causes a growth in your treasury.

Read this Psalm of thanks and from it will come other ways to worship the Lord.

> *"Give thanks to the LORD, call on his name; make known among the nations what he has done. Sing to him, sing praise to him; tell of all his wonderful acts. Glory in his holy name; let the hearts of those who seek the LORD rejoice. Look to the LORD and his strength; seek his face always. Remember the wonders he has done, his miracles, and the judgments he pronounced, O descendants of Israel his servant, O sons of Jacob, his chosen ones. He is the LORD our God; his judgments are in all the earth. He remembers his covenant forever, the word he commanded, for a thousand generations, the covenant he made with Abraham, the oath he swore to*

> Isaac. He confirmed it to Jacob as a decree, to Israel as an everlasting covenant: 'To you I will give the land of Canaan as the portion you will inherit.' When they were but few in number, few indeed, and strangers in it, they wandered from nation to nation, from one kingdom to another. He allowed no man to oppress them; for their sake he rebuked kings: 'Do not touch my anointed ones; do my prophets no harm. Sing to the LORD, all the earth; proclaim his salvation day after day. Declare his glory among the nations, his marvelous deeds among all peoples. For great is the LORD and most worthy of praise; he is to be feared above all gods. For all the gods of the nations are idols, but the LORD made the heavens. Splendor and majesty are before him; strength and joy in his dwelling place. Ascribe to the LORD, O families of nations, ascribe to the LORD glory and strength, ascribe to the LORD the glory due his name. Bring an offering and come before him; worship the LORD in the splendor of his holiness. Tremble before him, all the earth! The world is firmly established; it cannot be moved. Let the heavens rejoice, let the earth be glad; let them say among the nations, "The LORD reigns!" Let the sea resound, and all that is in it; let the fields be jubilant, and everything in them! Then the trees of the forest will sing, they will sing for joy before the LORD, for he comes to judge the earth. Give thanks to the LORD, for he is good; his love endures forever. Cry out, "Save us, O God our Savior; gather us and deliver us from the nations, that we may give thanks to your holy name, that we may glory in your praise." Praise be to the LORD, the God of Israel, from everlasting to everlasting. Then all the people said "Amen" and "Praise the LORD""*

(1 Chronicles 16:8-36).

3. Worship with Thanksgiving

> *"Give thanks to the Lord..."*

When you make thanksgiving a way of life, seeking every means through which you can offer thanks to God even for the daily routines of life, then you are worshipping the Lord with thanksgiving. There are too many things in a day for which you can thank the Lord. Even those things you might consider trivial, for them lift up your voice and thank the Lord.

You can thank Him for the oxygen
You can thank Him for the sunshine
You can thank Him for the rainfall
You can thank Him for your parents
You can thank Him for your siblings
You can thank Him for your spouse
You can thank Him for your children
You can thank Him for your job
You can thank Him for protection
You can thank Him for provision
You can thank Him for guidance
You can thank Him for your leaders; both political and spiritual leaders.
You can thank Him for your salvation.
Oh there are a thousand things you can thank God for daily.
Thank Him for your employer
Thank Him for your Boss
Thank Him for your employees
Thank Him for your subordinates
Thank Him for your brethren
Worship God with your thanksgiving!

4. Worship God by Calling His Names

"Call on His name".

When you call God by His names and attributes as revealed in the scriptures you are acknowledging who He is. That is also a form of worship. When you call Him Elohim you are acknowledging the fact that He is the Eternal Creator of all that is both visible and invisible. When you call Him Adonai you are acknowledging the fact that He is Sovereign over all, that all is under His sovereign rule and control. When you call Him EL Shaddai you acknowledge the fact that He is all sufficient and is more than enough for you. When you call Him ElOlam you are acknowledging that He is the everlasting God, that from eternity to eternity He remains God. You are acknowledging that He is the unchanging God. When you call Him Jireh you are saying He will meet all your needs. When you call Him Rohi, you are acknowledging the fact that He is your good Shepherd. When you call Him by His Names you trigger a revelation of Himself in the line of those names. You can worship God by just calling His names. Doing this tells the forces of evil that you know whom you have believed.

5. Worship God by Proclaiming His Deeds

"Make known among the nations what he has done"

When you give testimony of what the Lord has done it is a form of worship especially when you do it among the *"nations"* – those who do not know Him. God has not stopped working on your behalf. You can proclaim even His *"normal workings"* in your life. Worship the Lord by proclaiming His deeds to you and to your loved ones, etc.

6. Worship the Lord By Singing to Him

"Sing to Him, sing praise to Him; tell of all His wonderful acts."

What we do most of the time is to sing about God. In that way we may be proclaiming what He is or what He has done to others. But we can also sing to God. In fact, the Bible commands us to sing to Him. In singing to Him you can sing His praises or sing to Him what He has done for you, in you, or through you. This is another form of worship – singing to the Lord.

7. Worship the Lord By Taking Pride in His Name

"Glory in His holy name"

To glory in His holy name means to *"take pride"* that you are called by the name of the Lord. It means you should rejoice in the fact that you are a child of God. Rejoice in all what you have access to because of that Name He has given us to use. Rejoice in what you have become because of the power in His holy name. O that you may proclaim His name in every breathe you take. That consciously and unconsciously you may continuously breathe that name.

I personally proclaim the name of Jesus many times a day. When I enter my car or my office, I proclaim *"Jesus Christ is Lord of all the heavens and the earth, and He reigns eternally"*. Each time I open the door of my house I proclaim it. Many times in the course of the day I declare *"Blessed be the name of the LORD"*. When you give glory to His holy name you grow in exercising the authority that name carries.

8. Worship The Lord By Depending On Him

"Looking to the LORD and His strength; seek His face always".

Looking to the Lord talks of dependence on Him in everything and for everything. Man has the tendency to act independently of God. So in looking to the Lord and His strength you are acknowledging the fact that you cannot rely on human strength. Seeking His face always, talks of seeking His approval and guidance for everything and in everything.

There are many who claim to worship the Lord yet they take decisions independently as though He does not exist. Worshipping the LORD consist in depending on Him always.

9. Worship The Lord With Your Offering

"Bring an offering and come before Him; worship the Lord in the splendor of His holiness".

When you offer the Lord anything, no matter how small you are worshipping Him in the splendor of His holiness. Do you remember He told the Israelites that no one should appear before Him empty handed? *"No one is to appear before me empty-handed"* (Exodus 23:15b) so you can worship the Lord with what you offer Him.

10. Worship The Lord By Your Attitude

"Tremble before Him, all the earth!"

This does not imply you start shaking like trees and buildings do when there is earth tremor or a hurricane. No, it talks of an attitude which reflects a reverential fear and respect for God when you are in His presence. When you maintain an attitude of respect you are worshiping God. This does not talk of a sanctimonious look that makes you look miserable but rather a joyful respect that stems from the heart.

11. Worship The Lord By Your Posture

"Come let us bow down in worship, let us kneel before the LORD our Maker". (Psalm 95:6)

"Then king David went in and sat before the LORD..."
(2 Samuel 7:18a)

"All the Levites who were musicians--Asaph, Heman, Jeduthun and their sons and relatives--stood on the east side of the altar, dressed in fine linen and playing cymbals, harps and lyres. They were accompanied by 120 priests sounding trumpets."
(2 Chronicles 5:12)

By the posture you assume in God's presence you can also worship Him. The most common form is to bow down and kneel down before Him. You can also lie prostrate before Him. You can as well sit down and worship Him. You can stand up and worship Him. Whatever posture you assume with reverence and awe in your heart is accepted. However there are some postures you are *"forced"* to assume when His glory is made manifest. You can not help but fall prostrate before Him. You can make it a discipline, not a law, to always assume a posture of bowing or kneeling before Him in worship.

When To Worship

You can maintain an attitude of worship, that is, you can be in the spirit of worship throughout the day. It largely depends on you. There is no specific time to worship the Lord but early in the morning can be a good time for regular or formal worship. The Psalmist said, *"In the morning, O LORD, you hear my voice"* (Psalm 5:3a). Worship Him before you go to bed.

Looking at the lives of some Bible characters you will also understand that you can worship the Lord even in the face of calamity. Some people *"worship"* the Lord when all is well but complain when things seem not to go well. The Bible says, *"In everything give thanks"*. In fact both Job and David show us good examples to worship the Lord even in the face of calamity.

> *"At this, Job got up and tore his robe and shaved his head. Then he fell to the ground in worship"* (Job 1:20).

> *"After Nathan had gone home, the LORD struck the child that Uriah's wife had borne to David, and he became ill. David pleaded with God for the child. He fasted and went into his house and spent the nights lying on the ground. The elders of his household stood beside him to get him up from the ground, but he refused, and he would not eat any food with them.*
> *On the seventh day the child died. David's servants were afraid to tell him that the child was dead, for they thought, "While the child was still living, we spoke to David but he would not listen to us. How can we tell him the child is dead? He may do something desperate. David noticed that his servants were whispering among themselves and he realized the child was dead. "Is the child dead?" he asked.*
> *"Yes," they replied, "he is dead." Then David got up from the ground. After he had washed, put on lotions and changed his clothes, he went into the house of the LORD and worshiped. Then he went to his own house, and at his request they served him food, and he ate."* (2 Samuel 12:15-20)

Your worship will determine your growth and your growth is reflected in your worship.

CHAPTER 5

YOUR GROWTH IS DETERMINED BY, AND REFLECTED IN TRUSTWORTHINESS

The Bible says *"righteousness exalts a nation"*. When you are trustworthy in little things God will exalt you and promote you. In other words you will grow in all domains of your life. Many people want to grow into spiritual leadership but God will not allow them because they can not be trusted.

When Israel was in need of leaders, this is the recommendation that was given to Moses: *"But select capable men from all the people--men who fear God, trustworthy men who hate dishonest gain--and appoint them as officials over thousands, hundreds, fifties and tens."* (Exodus 18:21). How can you determine if a man is trustworthy or not?

Elements of Trustworthiness

1. **Fear of the Lord:**

The foundational element in the life of any trustworthy person is the fear of the Lord, because to *"fear the Lord is to shun evil"*.

2. **Hatred for dishonest gain**

For someone to be trustworthy, he must hate all manner of dishonest gain. The Lord can not promote you if you are dishonest in any way. In fact as soon as you become dishonest in any way, you stop growing. This is because dishonesty is inductive. If you are dishonest with little things you will also be dishonest with greater things.

"Whoever can be trusted with very little can also be trusted with much, and whoever is dishonest with very little will also be dishonest with much. So if you have not been trustworthy in handling worldly wealth, who will trust you with true riches? And if you have not been trustworthy with someone else's property, who will give you property of your own?" (Luke 16:10-12)

If you can be trusted with little, you can be trusted with much. If you are dishonest with little you will be dishonest with much.

If you want to grow into the true riches of the kingdom, you must be trustworthy with worldly wealth.

One of the characteristics Paul gave, for those who must rise to spiritual leadership is that they should be those *"not pursuing dishonest gain"* (see 1 Timothy 3:8, Titus 1:7).

If you are not trustworthy you will be capable of distorting the scripture and teaching things you ought not teach for the sake of dishonest gain. Doing this you will ruin the lives of many. *"For there are many rebellious people, mere talkers and deceivers, especially those of the circumcision group. They must be silenced, because they are ruining whole households by teaching things they ought not to teach--and that for the sake of dishonest gain"* (Titus 1:10-11).

3. **Ability to keep a secret:**
"A gossip betrays a confidence, but a trustworthy man keeps a secret" (Proverbs 11:13).

Trustworthiness implies being able to keep your mouth shut. As you grow spiritually many people will come and share very personal issues with you because they are in need of your prayers, counsel, or wisdom. You must be able to keep these things between you and them without letting others know. The moment you betray someone else's confidence your growth becomes retarded.

Actually, when you give information about A to B without A's permission, you are gossiping and thereby betraying A's trust. No body will share personal things about himself with you if he did not trust you. To now tell others is to betray that trust. When the Holy Spirit sees that you can keep a secret, He will raise to a position, and endow you with what it takes to be of help to people with very personal problems.

4. Diligence

"Like the coolness of snow at harvest time is a trustworthy messenger to those who send him; he refreshes the spirit of his masters." (Proverbs 25:13)

"Well done, my good servant!' his master replied. `Because you have been trustworthy in a very small matter, take charge of ten cities" (Luke 19:17)

Another element of trustworthiness is diligence. You can also trust a diligent person to put in his all in the execution of an assignment. A trustworthy messenger who is sent will also execute his assignment well and this brings joy to the heart of the one who sends him. In fact he will refresh the spirit of those who send him. After you have sent such a messenger you relax and are sure that he is going to do exactly what he was asked to, when he was asked to do it and how he was asked to do it.

There are people to whom you give a responsibility and you are sure that come what may they will carry it to the end. There are others who must be supervised by the second to see if at all they are doing the job. Such ones are not trustworthy because they are not diligent. They are eye servants. The Master in the above parable commended the servant as trustworthy because he put to effective use what was entrusted to him and brought back the full return.

Can you be one of them?

"All Judah brought the tithes of grain, new wine and oil into the storerooms. I put Shelemiah the priest, Zadok the scribe, and a Levite named Pedaiah in charge of the storerooms and made Hanan son of Zaccur, the son of Mattaniah, their assistant, because these men were considered trustworthy. They were made responsible for distributing the supplies to their brothers" (Nehemiah 13:12-13).

God is looking for people He can put in charge in His supply department, those who will have access into His store house. But He seeks those who are trustworthy, who will not use for themselves what is meant to be passed on to others. Can God put you in charge to distribute the supplies of your brethren? What have you done with the little He has entrusted to your hands already? If God should consider what He destined to pass through your hands to others will He increase it or reduce it?

Can you be put in charge of God's store rooms? If you should be put in charge will it be for your blessing and promotion or will it bring you a course and demotion? So many people have demoted themselves by their unfaithfulness.

> *"After the wall had been rebuilt and I had set the doors in place, the gatekeepers and the singers and the Levites were appointed. I put in charge of Jerusalem my brother Hanani, along with[n] Hananiah the commander of the citadel, because he was a man of integrity and feared God more than most men do. I said to them, "The gates of Jerusalem are not to be opened until the sun is hot. While the gatekeepers are still on duty, have them shut the doors and bar them. Also appoint residents of Jerusalem as guards, some at their posts and some near their own houses"* (Nehemiah 7:1-3).

Nehemiah put this people in charge because of their integrity i.e. their trustworthiness and fear of God. You too can grow to the level of "*being in charge*" of certain things in God's kingdom if you prove yourself trustworthy.

1. **Honest testimony**

"A truthful witness gives honest testimony, but a false witness tells lies" (Proverbs 12:17).

Another element of trustworthiness is honesty in speech. From the way a man reports on an issue you can determine his degree of trustworthiness. No one who tells lies or half-truths can be trusted. In fact such a person is dangerous and should be kept from every responsibility. If you can not trust a man's words then there is nothing about him which can be trusted. A man's words reveal what is in him. When his words are dishonest, he is dishonest to the core.

To be worthy of anything, you must earn it and prove it. To be trustworthy (worthy of trust) you must earn it and prove it by the elements outlined above.

Your growth is determined by your trustworthiness and your trustworthiness reflects your degree of growth.

CHAPTER 6

YOUR GROWTH IS DETERMINED BY, AND REFLECTED IN HUMILITY

In the Christian life, what determines your growth is not your position in society or in the church. It is not what you own that determines your growth. Your growth is determined by your God-content. How much of God you possess determines how much authority you have and can exercise in the spirit realm. It is not how many people you have at your command who determine how great you are but how many people you are willing to and are actually serving.

In order that this point be made clear so that timidity is not confused for humility, we are going to see ways in which humility is manifested. There are many proud people who appear timid yet there are many bold people who are very humble. Society today takes cowardice and timidity for humility. In looking for humility what are you to consider?

1. Consideration for others

"Do nothing out of selfish ambition or vain conceit, but in humility consider others better than yourselves." (Philippians 2:3)

One characteristic of a proud person is that he always thinks he can do it better. He always considers himself better that others and has the tendency to pick out the flaws in the actions of others. On the other hand the humble person knows what he is but decides to consider others better than himself. A timid person does not know himself and consequently does not believe in himself. However a humble person knows what or who he is but decides (an action of the will) to consider others better that himself. He gives others the opportunity to do what he is well capable of doing and even doing it better. A humble person is not selfish in his attitude towards others. In fact he gives out himself for the welfare of others. His decisions are taken and implemented with others in mind. He will allow others to serve themselves first even when he is rightfully the one to be served. A humble person does nothing with the intention of self-promotion.

2. Dependence on the Lord

> *"There, by the Ahava Canal, I proclaimed a fast, so that we might humble ourselves before our God and ask him for a safe journey for us and our children, with all our possessions"* (Ezra 8:21).

Another way in which humility is expressed is through a man's dependence on God. Humble people are prayerful people because they rely on God for everything. They will not hesitate to fast so that God intervenes rather than act on their own. Self sufficient people hardly pray because they do not see any need for God. You can measure your level of humility by the extent to which you can pray and fast for God's intervention on a particular issue.

3. Heart brokenness over the sins of others.

> *"I am afraid that when I come again my God will humble me before you, and I will be grieved over many who have sinned earlier and have not repented of the impurity, sexual sin and debauchery in which they have indulged"* (2 Corinthians 12:21).

Humility is expressed in heartbrokenness over the sins of others. Humble people do not rejoice when anyone *"falls"* into sin, not even those they consider *"rivals"* or *"enemies"*. This is because they know that it is not by their own strength that they stand. They do not even talk of the fact that the one who has *"fallen"* into that sin or the other deserves it because of this or that. Instead they grieve over the sins of others especially when the one who has sinned takes his or her sins lightheartedly. The Apostle Paul wrote, *"who is weak, and I do not feel weak? Who is led into sin, and I do not inwardly burn"?* (Colossians 11:29). People who are humble identify themselves with others in their weaknesses. They identify with others in their failures. They identify with others in their sins and grief.

When is the last time you grieved over the sinful attitude of someone? When is the last time you identified with someone in his or her weakness or failure. When did you last plead for the Lord to grant to someone a repentant heart that expresses brokenness over sin. No matter how arrogant that person may be in his or her sin do not wish him or her to come under judgment, intercede for him or her. In fact intercession is one of the ways in which humility is expressed.

4. Your reaction when treated unfairly

Some people have the appearance of the embodiment of humility. When you scratch them then you see the sleeping viper you were playing with. When you react to insults and retaliate when treated badly it portrays your lack of humility. Quiet people are not always humble people as many think. Some people appear quiet just because they have not gotten real opportunities to express their real nature.

Peter wrote, "Finally, all of you, live in harmony with one another; be sympathetic, love as brothers, be compassionate and humble. Do not repay evil with evil or insult with insult, but with blessing, because to this you were called so that you may inherit a blessing" (1 Peter 3:8-9).

Some people do not react immediately when they are treated unfairly but they do everything to paint the one who has maltreated them black before others. They will tell others of how that one has hurt them and most often go to exaggerations. Such are worse than the one who reacts immediately. Often those who react immediately bury the matter. However, it is better not to react and not to tell others about what happened. You can settle the matter peacefully and upfront with the one who has treated you unfairly.

5. Your attitude towards personal sin

You can tell your degree of humility by taking note of your reaction when confronted with personal sin. Some people react violently when confronted with their sin. Others labour to bring in all manner of justification as to why they sinned. A humble person does not mind who confronts him, or how he is confronted. His only response is to the truth. He acknowledges his sin and repents irrespective of the messengers' manner of approach. Some proud people think that there is a particular *"civil"* way they should be confronted with their sin. Such want to be pampered and treated with respect.

> *Now listen to this, "I am going to bring disaster on you. I will consume your descendants and cut off from Ahab every last male in Israel--slave or free. I will make your house like that of Jeroboam son of Nebat and that of Baasha son of Ahijah, because you have provoked me to anger and have caused Israel to sin. "And also concerning Jezebel the LORD says: 'Dogs will devour Jezebel by the wall of Jezreel.' Dogs will eat those belonging to Ahab who die in the city, and the birds of the air will feed on those who die in the country." (There was never a man like Ahab, who sold himself to do evil in the eyes of the LORD, urged on by Jezebel his wife. He behaved in the vilest manner by going after idols, like the Amorites the LORD drove out before Israel.) When Ahab heard these words, he tore his clothes, put on sackcloth and fasted. He lay in sackcloth and went around meekly. Then the word of the LORD came to Elijah the Tishbite: "Have you noticed how Ahab has humbled himself before me? Because he has humbled himself, I will not bring this disaster in his day, but I will bring it on his house in the days of his son."* (1 Kings 21:21-29)

In spite of Ahab's wickedness, his humility was expressed in his reaction when confronted with his personal sin. And God spared him the judgment that would have been released.

Now listen to another story and see the predicament of another king who reacted wrongly when confronted with his personal sin.

> *"But after Uzziah became powerful, his pride led to his downfall. He was unfaithful to the LORD his God and entered the temple of the LORD to burn incense on the altar of incense. Azariah the priest with eighty other courageous priests of the LORD followed him in. They confronted him and said, "It is not right for you,*

Uzziah, to burn incense to the LORD. That is for the priests, the descendants of Aaron, who have been consecrated to burn incense. Leave the sanctuary, for you have been unfaithful; and you will not be honored by the LORD God."
Uzziah, who had a censer in his hand ready to burn incense, became angry. While he was raging at the priests in their presence before the incense altar in the LORD's temple, leprosy broke out on his forehead. When Azariah the chief priest and all the other priests looked at him, they saw that he had leprosy on his forehead, so they hurried him out. Indeed, he himself was eager to leave, because the LORD had afflicted him. King Uzziah had leprosy until the day he died. He lived in a separate house --leprous and excluded from the temple of the LORD. Jotham his son had charge of the palace and governed the people of the land." (2 Chronicles 26:16-21)

6. Your attitude towards God's Word

"Because your heart was responsive, and you humbled yourself before God when you heard what he spoke against this place and its people, and because you humbled yourself before me and tore your robes and wept in my presence, I have heard you, declares the LORD." (2 Chronicles 34:27)

Another way in which humility is expressed is by a positive response to the word of God. Pride and hardness of heart go together. No hard-hearted person can be humble. In fact, hard heartedness is one of the chief manifestations of pride. When a man becomes indifferent to the word of God, he is just manifesting pride.

A humble person will always respond to God's word no matter who is proclaiming it. There is no way you can grow spiritually if you do not uphold the right attitude towards God's written or spoken word. When you concentrate on who says what rather than on what is said then like Balaam you will one day miss God's instruction on your path to destruction without remedy.

7. Your acknowledgement of God

> *"The leaders of Israel and the king humbled themselves and said, "The LORD is just" (2 Chronicles 12:6).*

When you see justice in all that God does or allows to happen, it is an expression of humility. There are some who think that God is unjust in permitting certain things to happen the way they happen. God is just in everything He does or allows to happen.

Another way of acknowledging the LORD is to see Him behind all your accomplishments. You come to the point where you realize that there is nothing in your life that you have done without His help. You come to the point where you acknowledge that without Him you can do nothing. Like Isaiah you can confidently say, without any regret, *"LORD you established peace for us; all that we have accomplished You have done for us"* (Isaiah 26:12). Acknowledge the Lord's hand in the little things that you consider routines. See His hand of enabling in all you are able to do actively or passively. That will be an expression of humility.

8. Your attitude towards promotion

You can also determine how humble you are by your reaction to spiritual promotion or commission. There are some who think that they are chosen because of who they are or what they have done. Such people look down on others whose turn for promotion has not yet come. Because God is using you today does not mean He will not use that other person tomorrow, and even in a greater measure.

Do not use promotion to try to lord it over others: God lifts you up for the uplifting of others. Do not think that it is because of your wisdom, or any such thing, that God is using you. In fact Moses told the Israelites,

> *"For you are a people holy to the LORD your God. The LORD your God has chosen you out of all the peoples on the face of the earth to be his people, his treasured possession.*
> *The LORD did not set his affection on you and choose you because you were more numerous than other peoples, for you were the fewest of all peoples. But it was because the LORD loved you and kept the*

oath he swore to your forefathers that he brought you out with a mighty hand and redeemed you from the land of slavery, from the power of Pharaoh king of Egypt" (Deuteronomy 7:6-8)

Read the reaction of different servants of God when they received a promotion from the LORD.

- Moses

"But Moses said to God, "Who am I that I should go to Pharaoh and bring the Israelites out of Egypt?" (Exodus 3:11)

- Gideon

"But Lord, " Gideon asked, "how can I save Israel? My clan is the weakest in Manasseh, and I am the least in my family." (Judges 6:15)

- Saul

"Saul answered, "But am I not a Benjamite, from the smallest tribe of Israel, and is not my clan the least of all the clans of the tribe of Benjamin? Why do you say such a thing to me?" (1 Samuel 9:21)

- David

"But David said to Saul, "Who am I, and what is my family or my father's clan in Israel, that I should become the king's son-in-law?" (1 Samuel 18:18) (2 Samuel 7:18)

- Solomon

"Now, O LORD my God, you have made your servant king in place of my father David. But I am only a little child and do not know how to carry out my duties" (1 King 3:7)

- Isaiah

"Woe to me!" I cried. "I am ruined! For I am a man of unclean lips, and I live among a people of unclean lips, and my eyes have seen the King, the LORD Almighty." (Isaiah 6:5)

- Jeremiah

"Ah, Sovereign LORD," I said, "I do not know how to speak; I am only a child." (Jeremiah 1:6)

- Peter

"When Simon Peter saw this, he fell at Jesus' knees and said, "Go away from me, Lord; I am a sinful man!" (Luke 5:8)

The Effects of Humility

1. **It guarantees Divine habitation**

   "For this is what the high and lofty One says-- He who lives forever, whose name is holy: "I live in a high and holy place, but also with him who is contrite and lowly in spirit, to revive the spirit of the lowly and to revive the heart of the contrite" (Isaiah 57:15).

   To be lowly in spirit and to be contrite in heart are all signs of humility. The extent to which you are humble is the extent to which you provide God with a dwelling place. And it is the presence of God in your life which guarantees a healthy growth in all aspects of life.

2. **It gives you worth in God's sight**

   "This is the one I esteem: he who is humble and contrite in spirit, and trembles at my word" (Isaiah 66:2b).

   Do you want to be of worth in the sight of the Almighty God, possessor of heaven and earth? Then humility is the key to that. God esteems those who are humble. When God esteems you, you become His treasured possession, like the apple of His eye. In fact when He esteems you He takes upon Himself to provide for you, protect you, preserve you, promote you, and prosper you.

3. **It guarantees your uplifting**

   "Humble yourselves, therefore, under God's mighty hand, that he may lift you up in due time" (1 Peter 5:6).

   If you humble yourself, then God will surely lift you up. In other words if you want to receive divine uplifting, then self-abasement is the pathway. The only way to guarantee your Divine uplifting is by humbling yourself. You can not exalt yourself, you cannot promote yourself. Actually any form of self-exaltation or self-promotion is the shortest cut to the lowest bottom. But self-abasement and self-effacement are the shortest cuts to the topmost top. This is because *"No one from the east or the west or from the desert can exalt a man. But it is God who judges: He brings one down, he exalts another"* (Psalm 75:6-7).

4. It triggers the flow of Grace

"Young men, in the same way be submissive to those who are older. All of you, clothe yourselves with humility toward one another, because, "God opposes the proud but gives grace to the humble" (1 Peter 5:5).

Thus the extent of your humility will determine your degree of growth and your growth will be reflected in your humility as per its different expressions given earlier on in this chapter.

We have come to the end of the first part which treated the aspect of growth. Each of the above factors will enhance your growth in whatever you do in this Christian life. There must be a careful and balanced application of each of the factors to ensure a proper and balanced growth.

Remember we looked at how Giving (Generosity) affects growth. We also looked at Reading (Research) and saw how it determines growth. We talked of obedience (observance) as the bedrock of growth. Next, we looked at Worship as an essential factor to growth. We also looked at Trustworthiness and saw how it determines growth. Finally, we have seen how humility will enhance growth.

In summary, growth consists of:
Giving
Reading
Worship
Obedience
Trustworthiness
Humility

Having known this you can determine how fast and how healthy you will grow. The Lord bless you as you apply these.

Part Two

CHAPTER 7

MATURITY

In this section we are going to look at MATURITY.

One way of understanding something is to understand what it is not. Hence to understand maturity we shall look at what maturity is not. That is, we will begin by looking at immaturity. We shall look at behaviours, attitudes and tendencies which characterise immaturity. Though growth is a necessary condition for maturity, it is not a sufficient condition. There are many grown ups who are immature to the core. The fact that you are grown up does not automatically qualify you for maturity. There are things which you must eliminate in order to become mature and there are things which you must do to enhance maturity. Spiritually speaking there are infants – the immature and there are adults – the mature. The Apostle John talked of the children, the youths and the elders.

The Apostle Paul said: *"We do, however, speak a message of wisdom among the mature, but not the wisdom of this age or of the rulers of this age, who are coming to nothing"* (1 Corinthians 2:6). If there are things which can only be spoken among the mature, it means there are some who are immature, unqualified to hear certain things. There is a message of wisdom which can only be spoken to the mature. That is why it is a tragedy to remain spiritually immature. You deprive yourself of many things by clinging to babyhood.

What then are the characteristics of immaturity?

"Brothers, I could not address you as spiritual but as worldly--mere infants in Christ. I gave you milk, not solid food, for you were not yet ready for it. Indeed, you are still not ready. You are still worldly. For since there is jealousy and quarreling among you, are you not worldly? Are you not acting like mere men? For when one says, "I follow Paul," and another, "I follow Apollos," are you not mere men?" (1 Corinthians 3:1-4)

Paul wrote to the Corinthians rebuking them for their immaturity. From the above passage maturity is manifested in.

1. Jealousy:

Jealousy is ill will harboured against someone because of what the person is or what he has. You know even in the natural an infant can become readily jealous of his mate when the latter is shown some favour he thinks he deserves. At times they harbour intense ill-will just because a mate owns something they can not own.

If there is any trace of jealousy in your heart, it is an indication of immaturity. Eliminating it will help set you on course to maturity.

2. Quarrelling:

Mature people are people of few words of great impact. A sign of immaturity is uncontrolled talking. And quarrelling is talking without control. When you have the tendency to answer back before you have listened, it is a sign of immaturity. Mature people wait to be given the opportunity to talk. Some people always interrupt others to make their point. This is another sign of gross immaturity.

3. Not seeing beyond the human:

Some people have the tendency to classify servants of God. Their focus is on men rather on God who commissioned those men and is working through them. Such people take pride in one servant of God over another forgetting that men are only servants of a great God. You know for some people, though X may say something by the spirit, their hearts are closed until Y says the same thing. They are prejudiced in their heart and such can easily be derailed to accept anything Y says even when it is contrary to sound doctrine.

4. Easily led into sin:

> *"But if anyone causes one of these little ones who believe in me to sin, it would be better for him to have a large millstone hung around his neck and to be drowned in the depths of the sea."* (Matthew 18:6)

Children can easily be led into doing what they might not want to do. You just need to know the words to use or the favour to show a child and he will do what he knows very well is wrong. It is the same thing in the spiritual. Those who are easily led into sin do not do it because they are unaware that their words or actions are wrong but because of their immaturity they lack the capacity to say *"no"* and hold to it.

When you can be induced by another person to say what you know is wrong or do what you know is wrong then you are immature. Most often, children don't sin on their own initiative but are induced by others to do the wrong thing. That is why a child's company matters a lot.

> *"Then we will no longer be infants, tossed back and forth by the waves, and blown here and there by every wind of teaching and by the cunning and craftiness of men in their deceitful scheming."* (Ephesians 4:14)

5. Instability in faith:

Infants are unstable in their faith. They can easily be knocked off course by waves. The life of an infant is characterised by doubts. Today he trusts God for this, tomorrow he doesn't know if God will answer. That is a sign of immaturity.

6. Instability in belief:

"Blown here and there by every wind of teaching…" infants have the tendency to be carried away and believing everything without testing it and searching the scriptures. They are easily carried away by

any new teaching in the air especially when it appeals to their heart's inclination. You have the right and the responsibility to authenticate any teaching by cross examining it in light of the Bible's stand point and what other authorities have said on the subject.

If today your view on this issue is X, tomorrow it is Y, another day it is Z, and still another time you do not even know where you belong, it just shows how immature you are.

7. Moving according to circumstances:

"... Tosses back and forth by the waves"

The waves here represent the dictates of circumstances. Those who are immature respond to and live their lives based on the circumstances surrounding them. Their choices depend on circumstances. Their commitment depends on circumstance. They are *"fair weather Christians"*. You can count on them when all around them is fine. When things become a little uncomfortable they become most unreliable. The bible likens such people to intermittent streams.

"But my brothers are as undependable as intermittent streams, as the streams that overflow when darkened by thawing ice and swollen with melting snow, but that cease to flow in the dry season, and in the heat vanish from their channels. Caravans turn aside from their routes; they go up into the wasteland and perish. The caravans of Tema look for water, the traveling merchants of Sheba look in hope. They are distressed, because they had been confident; they arrive there, only to be disappointed. Now you too have proved to be of no help; you see something dreadful and are afraid" (Job 6:15-21).

8. They expect others to dance to the tune of their music:

"To what can I compare this generation? They are like children sitting in the marketplaces and calling out to others:
"We played the flute for you, and you did not dance; we sang a dirge, and you did not mourn" (Matthew 11:16-17).

Children always expect others to follow the tune of their music whether it is appealing or not. To them as long as the flute is played everyone should dance to the tune of it even if they have to dance out of rhythm. They want everybody to mourn when a dirge is song even if the person is not concerned.

Are you one who expects everybody around you to be cold and sad just because you are cold and sad? You want to become everybody's standard. Because you are happy you expect everybody to be happy. Because you are displeased with something everybody should be displeased with it. Because you are appreciative of someone you expect everybody to be appreciative of the person or his actions. This is a sign of gross immaturity. Mature people know that everyone has a right to choose and to express his own opinion. They take no offence when someone else's opinion is different or even contrary to theirs.

9. They judge others according to their own opinions:

"For John came neither eating nor drinking, and they say, 'He has a demon.' The Son of Man came eating and drinking, and they say, 'Here is a glutton and a drunkard, a friend of tax collectors and "sinners."' But wisdom is proved right by her actions" (Matthew 11:18-19).

People who are often highly opinionated are those who are immature. They judge and classify people according to their opinion about the people or about an aspect in question. In the passage above the Lord Jesus Christ likened that generation to children because they thought their opinion is the basis for judging or classifying people. Mature people have the word of God as the final authority in judging their actions or those of others. They know that the only thing that counts is what God's word says about the person or the thing in question. They are ready at any given moment to discard their opinions as soon as it is made clear to them that such opinions are not founded on God's word.

Immature people on the other hand hold to their opinions until they reap the bitter consequences of wrong opinions.

10. They are easily embittered and discouraged:

"Fathers, do not embitter your children, or they will become discouraged" (Colossians 3:21).

There is a point in life where anyone can be prone to discouragement. But children in particular are easily given to discouragement. In fact, often you will have to encourage children to do even things that benefit nobody else but them.

Spiritual babies must be encouraged to eat for their own spiritual wellbeing. They must be encouraged to attend meetings. The slightest thing that happens to them gets them discouraged no matter how important what they are doing is. Their commitment to God or the things of God depends on how others behave towards them. That is why some spiritual babies move from one assembly to another. They leave from here because they think someone in particular has not treated them well. This is also because children are not committed to anything. So when they leave nothing is affected. If they were committed, they would consider the work of God that will be affected if they leave, hence encourage themselves to move on.

That is why Paul admonishes parents (those who are mature) not to embitter children (the immature). He says it again in Ephesians 6:4a *"Father, do not exasperate your children".*

11. They want to choose first:

Another manifestation of immaturity is the desire to be the first to choose. Children do not consider others but always want to satisfy themselves before others can be served. You know when a mother cooks in the house, in the case where the food might not be enough for everybody she serves all to the members of her household even if she has to go hungry. But when a child cooks she serves herself even before the head of the house is served.

Lot manifested his immaturity in deciding to choose his own portion of the land before his uncle who brought him up.

12. They are slow to learn:

"We have much to say about this, but it is hard to explain because you are slow to learn. 12 In fact, though by this time you ought to be teachers, you need someone to teach you the elementary truths of God's word all over again. You need milk, not solid food! Anyone who lives on milk, being still an infant, is not acquainted with the teaching about righteousness" (Hebrews 5:11-13).

Children are very slow to learn. You will have to explain one thing over and over before a child understands. At times you are forced to use different methods to explain the same thing to communicate to the child.

Spiritual babies too are slow to learn spiritual truths. Spiritual babies always want to hear things they are accustomed to hearing. They linger around the elementary truths. In fact they take offence when deep things are taught because to them they appear as nonsense. If you are slow in grasping spiritual truths, then you have an immature spiritual brain. You are still a spiritual baby. Babies want to be taught on God's love and the availability of grace continuously. They take offence when you confront them with teachings on righteousness, holiness, sacrifice and judgement.

13. They lack discernment:

"But solid food is for the mature, who by constant use have trained themselves to distinguish good from evil" (Hebrews 5:13).
"Even a child is known by his actions, by whether his conduct is pure and right" (Proverbs 20:11).

You can easily identify a child by his or her actions and mannerisms no matter his size or age. Children do things not based on whether they are right or wrong but because they feel like doing them. This is because they have not trained themselves to distinguish what is right from what is wrong. They are unable to discern the consequences of their actions. Mature people evaluate and sample their actions based on the knowledge of whether they are good or evil. They evaluate their words based on whether they are good or evil not according to their feelings. When you do things or say things according to your feelings and not based on their right or wrong, good or evil nature, then you are still an infant. These are all characteristics of immaturity. In this light, Paul said, *"When I was a child, I talked like a child, I reasoned like a child. When I became a man, I put childish ways behind me"* (1 Corinthians 13:11).

If you must grow into maturity you must put all those childish ways (behaviour, attitudes, actions, and tendencies) behind you. After you have put them behind, you now forget what is behind and strain towards what is ahead. That is, you now begin to work towards maturity.

What then is Maturity?

1. It is to have full assurance

> *"Epaphras, who is one of you and a servant of Christ Jesus, sends greetings. He is always wrestling in prayer for you, that you may stand firm in all the will of God, mature and fully assured"* (Colossians 4:12).

Maturity is to take your stand in all that you know to be the will of God for you. It is taking a firm stand in the things of God. Epaphras prayed for the Colossian church to become mature by standing firm in all the will of God. This is what brings full assurance in the life of the believer. Mature people are always fully assured of their stand in the Lord. They are not moved by circumstances or winds of doctrine.

> *Paul said, "Not that I have already obtained all this, or have already been made perfect, but I press on to take hold of that for which Christ Jesus took hold of me. Brothers, I do not consider myself yet to have taken hold of it. But one thing I do: Forgetting what is behind and straining toward what is ahead, I press on*

> *toward the goal to win the prize for which God has called me heavenward in Christ Jesus.*
> *All of us who are mature should take such a view of things. And if on some point you think differently, that too God will make clear to you. Only let us live up to what we have already attained."*
>
> (Philippians 3:12-16)

2. It is knowledge that you have not yet arrived

> *"But I press on to take hold..."*

When a man knows that he is not yet perfect, he will watch and discipline himself the more. I have come to realise that great men of God work the hardest. They are those who press on the most. Why? Because their sense of maturity cause them to know that there is still much left to be done in their calling and perfection as saints.

3. It is forgetting the past:

> *"Forgetting what is behind..."*

Mature people forget the past. They forget their past failures. They forget their past wounds. They forget their past victories and successes. Some people always talk of the past disappointments, fears and hurts. Mature people forget the past and strain towards their goal. They do not allow themselves to be distracted from their goal.

4. It is living up to what you have attained:

> *"Only let us live up to what we have attained".*

This talks of obeying all you know there is to obey. To know a truth and not live up to it is not a sign of maturity. Maturity is converting head knowledge to heart knowledge and allowing it to become a life experience.

5. It is living in the fullness of Christ:

> *"...until we all reach unity in the faith and in the knowledge of the Son of God and become mature, attaining to the whole measure of the fullness of Christ"* (Ephesians 4:13).

> *"Perseverance must finish its work so that you may be mature and complete, not lacking anything"* (James 1:4).

What does it mean to attain to the whole measure of the fullness of Christ? It is when we come to the point where Christ is our sufficiency. Where you actually genuinely see yourself as *"complete, not lacking anything"*, then that is maturity. When you come to this point, nothing else satisfies you but a full devotion to God. Everything is done to lead you to the fullness of the knowledge of Him who died and rose again. It is living a life void of worries, anxieties and pleasures (Luke 8:14). You ought to see yourself complete in Christ. See yourself as not lacking anything because everything in heaven has been made available to you in Christ Jesus.

6. It is living so that your life becomes an example:

> *"Don't let anyone look down on you because you are young, but set an example for the believers in speech, in life, in love, in faith and in purity"* (1 Timothy 4:12).

Those who are mature live so as to be an example for others to emulate.

When they speak they are aware that their manner of speech can be emulated by somebody.

They live and model their life in such a way that nobody who blindly follows them will be led astray. They set examples through their acts of love. They are examples in faith and in purity. That is what maturity is all about.

7. It is the product of perseverance:

> *"Perseverance must finish its work so that you may be mature and complete, not lacking anything"* (James 1:4).
> *"But the seed on good soil stands for those with a noble and good heart, who hear the word, retain it, and by persevering produce a crop"* (Luke 8:15).

The work of perseverance is to lead to maturity. Without perseverance there can be no maturity. Plants are considered mature when they produce crops which can be harvested by the farmer. To get to this stage the plant must have gone through adverse environmental conditions. Those who have gone through storms in life manifest a degree of maturity unlikely to be manifested by those who have not. Those who have persevered adverse or harsh conditions in life carry on them an air of maturity that those who have had it easy throughout do not carry.

This is because maturity is a product of perseverance. That is why people who easily give up and fail to hold through storms remain babies all their lives. No matter how old they are in the Christian life, the quota of maturity produced by perseverance will be missing in their lives.

8. It is speaking the truth in love

"Then we will no longer be infants, tossed back and forth by the waves, and blown here and there by every wind of teaching and by the cunning and craftiness of men in their deceitful scheming. Instead, speaking the truth in love, we will in all things grow up into him who is the Head, that is, Christ" (Ephesians 4:14-15).

When people are mature they are honest and transparent. They speak the truth even when it hurts. They do so out of love, with no intention of hurting the other but of bringing the best out of him.

Factors that Influence Maturity:

Now we are going to look at the factors which influence and reflect maturity. Like growth, there are factors which influence a man's maturity, which is reflected in these same factors. A proper understanding and application of these factors will greatly enhance your degree of maturity. There is no need growing without maturing. The purpose of growth is to lead to maturity which leads to fruits bearing. Farmers, during harvest, are out for what a plant has produced through its maturity and not how big the plant has grown. In fact the bigger the plant is without maturity the more it offends the farmer.

We are going to use the letters of the word maturity to bring out vital lessons:

Meditations
Affection
Teachability
Understanding
Responsibility
Initiative
Trust
Yielding/ ability to yield

CHAPTER 8

YOUR DEGREE OF MATURITY IS DETERMINED BY, AND REFLECTED IN, YOUR MEDITATIONS

"For as he thinketh in his heart so is he" (Proverbs 23:7a).

By meditations we mean the things you allow your heart to think about. Those things you allow your heart or mind to dwell on are your meditations. And they determine how mature you become. You can only rise as far as your meditations take you. No other thing determines your productivity like your meditations.

1. Your meditations determine your demeanour:

"How long must I wrestle with my thoughts
and every day have sorrow in my heart?
How long will my enemy triumph over me?" (Psalm 13:2)

Whether a man is sorrowful or joyful does not actually depend much on what happens on the outside of him but on what is happening on his inside. Your meditations determine whether you carry a joyful disposition or a sorrowful one. When you allow your mind and heart to dwell on the goodness of the Lord you will always be joyful as your heart will be full of gratitude to God.

However when you focus on the things which are lacking then sorrow will be your portion. The fact that David wrestled with his thoughts shows that the thoughts were not right. And at the end all they could bring him was sorrow in his heart. You do not need to struggle with your thoughts. The easiest way to deal with negative thoughts is to dwell on positive things. Let your mind be focused on good things. Because your meditations determine your demeanour and your demeanour affects everything around you, your productivity is also greatly affected. And your maturity is reflected in your productivity.

Also when you allow your mind to dwell on the negative you make yourself vulnerable to defeat. That is why David asks *"How long will my enemy triumph over me?"*

2. Your meditations determine your insight:

"I have more insight than all my teachers, for I meditate on your statutes" (Psalm 119:99).

Meditation on the statutes of God is what gives you insight into kingdom mysteries. Insight into kingdom mysteries is not a function of one's spiritual age but of one's life of meditation. There is insight that you can never have from casual reading of the scriptures. No-one can teach or impart this insight to you. It is the result of meditating on the word of God. Again David said, *"Your commands make me wiser than my enemies, for they are ever with me"*.

3. Your meditations determine your love for the word:

"Oh how I love your law! I mediate on it all day long"

You want to love God's word? Then meditate on it. As you meditate on the word, it gives you insight into kingdom mysteries. Meditation on the word will cause you to fall for it a thousand times over. As you meditate on the word, it gives answers to every puzzle of life. In fact you become a master at balancing the equations of life. Everybody loves what provides solution to his problems. And the word is a guaranteed solution provider to those who take time to search for the answers.

4. Your meditations determine your choices:

"I meditate on your precepts and consider your ways" (Psalm119:15).

"Though rulers sit together and slander me, your servant will meditate on your decrees. Your statutes are my delight; they are my counselors" (Psalm119:23-24).

As you mediate on the word of God, it leads you to consider His ways in every choice you want to make. The word will give you counsel in whatever you are engaged in and lead you to choose rightly. However, this only happens as you meditate on it. The Holy Spirit who is the counsellor will use the word to give you counsel as you meditate. God speaks to us primarily through His word. As you meditate on the word you will receive counsel with respect to your choices in life.

5. Your mediations determine your confidence:

"Though rulers sit together and slander me, your servant will meditate on your decrees" (Psalm 119:23).
"May the arrogant be put to shame for wronging me without cause; but I will meditate on your precepts" (Psalm 119:78).

Those who meditate on God's word have their confidence in God. They are not moved by the people who are gathered against them. They are unperturbed by those who slander them and maltreat them. They can always confidently ask, *"Why do the nations conspire and the peoples plot in vain? The kings of the earth rise up and the rulers band together against the Lord and against his anointed"* (Psalm 2:1-2 KJV). Then they join the One enthroned to laugh at those who are gathered against them, *"The One enthroned in heaven laughs; the Lord scoffs at them."* (Psalm 2:4). This is because they know that there is no plan which can succeed against the Almighty or against His anointed.

6. Your meditations determine your fruitfulness:

"Blessed is the man who does not walk in the counsel of the wicked or stand in the way of sinners or sit in the seat of mockers. But his delight is in the law of the LORD, and on his law he meditates day and night. He is like a tree planted by streams of water, which yields its fruit in season and whose leaf does not wither. Whatever he does prospers" (Psalm 1:1-3).

When you meditate on God's word, you will be led to make the right choices. You will distant yourself from evil companions and be established in Christ. This will make you fruitful and prosperous. Your prosperity will not be determined by circumstances because you will be like a tree whose leaves do not wither even in times of drought, reason being that you will be constantly watered by the word of God on which you mediate continuously. Whatever you do prospers and you will yield your fruits in season. Fruit here depicts success in all you do and prosperity in all aspects of your life because you will discover hidden secrets in the word. Joshua 1:8 connotes what we are saying here.

We have seen the effects of meditation. Now the question arises as to what one should meditate on.

What to Meditate on

1. Meditate on God's word

"Do not let this Book of the Law depart from your mouth; meditate on it day and night, so that you may be careful to do everything written in it. Then you will be prosperous and successful" (Joshua 1:8).

"I meditate on your precepts and consider your ways" (Psalm 119:15).

2. Meditate on God's love

"Within your temple, O God, we meditate on your unfailing love" (Psalm 48:9).

As you meditate (think about, allow your heart to dwell on God's unfailing love, you will in turn pour out your love to Him. As you meditate on God's unfading love for you praise and worship will flow from the deepest recesses of your heart unto the throne of grace.

3. Meditate on His works

"I will meditate on all your works and consider all your mighty deeds" (Psalm 77:12).

"I remember the days of long ago; I meditate on all your works and consider what your hands have done" (Psalm 143:5 KJV).

As you mediate on that which God has done in your life and in the lives of others you become confident that nothing is impossible with God. This will lead you to testify of His deeds.

4. Mediate on His wonders

"Let me understand the teaching of your precepts; then I will meditate on your wonders" (Psalm 119:27).

One of the most evident and closest wonders of the Lord is His creation. When you look at nature and the universe as a whole it tells you how great God is. Expose your heart often to nature. You can go into the forest or to gardens or to seasides and just bask yourself in nature. This increases your awe and reverence for the creator of the universe.

You can also meditate on the wonders of God by reading scientific articles and magazines concerning the solar system and outer space in general. Read articles that elaborate on the complexity of the human body. This will give you a renewed respect for the omniscient God, Creator of heaven and earth. Abraham called Him the Possessor of heaven and earth. I like that one! God almighty is the Possessor of heaven and earth. Whatever realm in this universe satan may lay claim to, it is only temporary because we give it to him.

5. Mediate on that which God has endowed you with

(1 Timothy 4:14-16 KJV)

When you think often about God's gifts to you, it will lead you to develop them. Meditation will also release the gifts in you which are hidden. The reason many people do not put to use God's gifts in them is because they do not meditate on the gifts. Meditating on the gifts will fan them and cause you to give yourself wholly to the work of God.

6. Meditate on the LORD

(Psalm 63:6 KJV)

You meditate on the LORD by focusing your mind and your heart on Him. You think of Him often. Think of His person, His character and attributes.

There is a price to pay

Everything in the Christian life has a price tag. To reap the benefits of meditation you have to pay a price:

a. **Looking for a quiet place and quiet time**

   "And Isaac went out to meditate in the field at the eventide" (Genesis 24:63a)

   The reason Isaac went into the field was so that the distractions at home would not affect him. Surely his father had many servants who would need his attention from time to time. He had to pay the price of seclusion by retreating from his normal activities in the cool of the evening in order to meditate.

b. **Burn the midnight oil**

   "When I remember thee upon my bed, and meditate on thee in the night watches" (Psalm 63:6 KJV).

   "My eyes stay open through the watches of the night, that I may meditate on your promises" (Psalm 119:148).

   You will have to stay awake or get up deep into the night in order to meditate. You will have to refuse yourself some hours of sleep so you can have time to mediate on the word of God.

CHAPTER 9

YOUR MATURITY IS DETERMINED BY, AND REFLECTED IN YOUR ATTITUDE

One's attitude towards certain aspects in life does not only reflect one's degree of maturity but is also a determinant factor of how mature that individual becomes. Infants have different attitudes towards different things in life than gown-ups do. Even among grown-ups, different attitudes will reflect different degrees of maturity. Maturity is independent of size or age. Maturity is not determined by physical or spiritual age. Your attitude greatly determines how mature you become or also tells your position on the ladder of maturity. Let us look at different attitudes which reflects or determines one's maturity.

Your Attitude Towards the Weak

Our attitude towards the weak and their weaknesses reflects how mature we are and also determine how mature we will become in life. Weaknesses vary from person to person, circumstances to circumstances and also from environment to environment. You must begin by knowing and understanding someone's personality and background, that is, knowing and understanding where he/she is coming from. This will go a long way to influence your attitude towards him or her.

We all come from different backgrounds. We have been affected by different people and different situations in life and therefore we react differently. What does the Lord expect of you with respect to your attitude towards the weak?

1. Accept The Weak

> *"Accept him whose faith is weak, without passing judgment on disputable matters. One man's faith allows him to eat everything, but another man, whose faith is weak, eats only vegetables"* (Romans 14:1-2).

Like I said earlier, we all come from different family, cultural, tribal, racial, academic, professional or social backgrounds. Where someone is coming from always, to some extend, have an influence on almost everything he does. From his choices, priorities, propensities, values, behaviour, speech etc. All these also have a bearing on that person's faith.

There are standards in the Christian life which we know cannot be compromised. They are indisputable matters. Nevertheless there are people who are weak and find themselves helpless before certain situations. Now instead of condemning someone who already admits his or her weakness and is willing to come out of it, the Bible says you should accept that individual. You do all in your power to see that the person does not feel condemned. When a man, who is born again, sees that he has been accepted in-spite of his weakness, he will do all to cooperate to see that that weakness is overcome; whatever it may be.

There are also things in the Christian life which the Bible terms *"disputable matters"*. In such matters, people's position obviously vary according to their background, for example, when it comes to the issue of make-up for women, this is a disputable matter and one's inclination as well as her background will determine one's position. Now a woman who does not make-up should accept the one who does and vice versa, likewise the issue of trousers for women.

Some other disputable issues are those of alcohol and tobacco. Some people abandon these immediately they believe. For others it takes time and there is need for deliverance to be administered to such (especially for those who had become addicts). Acceptance means you make room in your heart for those who differ with you in disputable issues.

2. Have Regard For The Weak

To have regard for the weak is to live your life in consideration of the weak. It is to think, speak, and act with the consciousness that there are some around you who might not be as strong as you are. It is to dress and comfort yourself in such a way that you do not become a stumbling block to someone because of his or her weakness.
Paul said, "Therefore let us stop passing judgment on one another. Instead, make up your mind not to put any stumbling block or obstacle in your brother's way" (Romans 14:13).

You have to make up your mind; you have to decide that your words, actions or even attitude will not influence someone negatively. That is why he could say *"Let us therefore make every effort to do what leads to peace and mutual edification"* (v 19).

In this light every word or action of yours should be judged on the basis of its capacity to edify. *"For it is better not to **eat** meat or **drink** wine or to **do anything** else that will cause your brother to fall"* (v 21) and again *"Therefore, if what I eat causes my brother to fall into sin, I will never eat meat again, so that I will not cause him to fall."* (1 Corinthians 8:13). When you live in that manner you are living with regard for the weak and the Lord says
- you are blessed
- the Lord will deliver you in times of trouble
- the Lord will protect you
- the Lord will preserve your life
- the Lord will not surrender you to the desire of your enemies
- the Lord will sustain you
- the Lord will restore you.

All the above blessings will enhance your climb on the maturity ladder.

3. Bear With The Weak

> *"We who are strong ought to bear with the failings of the weak and not to please ourselves"* (Romans 15:1).

There are certain things that the weaknesses of some people will lead them to do which can be very offensive and provocative. In such cases the Bible says you should bear with the failings of the weak. Live with others knowing that we have not yet attained perfection. That is why it is written: *"Brothers, if someone is caught in a sin, you who are spiritual should restore him gently. But watch yourself, or you also may be tempted. Carry each other's burdens, and in this way you will fulfill the law of Christ"* (Galatians 6:1-2).

Instead of rejection and condemnation the Bible says you should seek for how to restore that one gently. Again the Bible says,

> *"Bear with each other and forgive whatever grievances you may have against one another. Forgive as the Lord forgave you. And over all these virtues put on love, which binds them all together in perfect unity"* (Colossians 3:13-14).

> *"Above all, love each other deeply, because love covers over a multitude of sins"* (1 Peter 4:8).

4. Identify With The Weak

> *"To the weak I became weak, to win the weak. I have become all things to all men so that by all possible means I might save some"* (1 Corinthians 9:22).

> *"If one part suffers, every part suffers with it"* (1 Corinthians 12:26a).

Identifying yourself with the weak means considering their weakness as yours. The Master showed us this example when He decided to take on humanity. For Christ to have been able to sympathize with our weakness He had to identify Himself with us in our weakness.

> *"In bringing many sons to glory, it was fitting that God, for whom and through whom everything exists, should make the author of their salvation perfect through suffering. Both the one who makes men holy and those who are made holy are of the same family. So*

> *Jesus is not ashamed to call them brothers... Since the children have flesh and blood, he too shared in their humanity so that by his death he might destroy him who holds the power of death--that is, the devil-- and free those who all their lives were held in slavery by their fear of death. For surely it is not angels he helps, but Abraham's descendants. For this reason he had to be made like his brothers in every way, in order that he might become a merciful and faithful high priest in service to God, and that he might make atonement for" the sins of the people. Because he himself suffered when he was tempted, he is able to help those who are being tempted"*
> (Hebrews 2:10-11, 14-18).
>
> *"For we do not have a high priest who is unable to sympathize with our weaknesses, but we have one who has been tempted in every way, just as we are--yet was without sin." (Hebrews 4:15)*

If you too have to be able to influence the weak and help them, you have to identify yourself with them.

5. Help The Weak

> *"In everything I did, I showed you that by this kind of hard work we must help the weak, remembering the words the Lord Jesus himself said: "It is more blessed to give than to receive"* (Acts 20:35).
>
> *"And we urge you, brothers, warn those who are idle, encourage the timid, help the weak, be patient with everyone"* (1 Thessalonians 5:14).

Helping the weak is a must for the believer. You have to look for ways through which you can help those who are spiritually weak by strengthening them (Ezekiel 34:4). You can strengthen the spiritually weak by encouraging them, by teaching them, by praying with them and for them.

There are others who are financially weak. You can help them start something from which they can earn a living. Those who are materially weak, you can help by providing for some of their basic needs.

Again the LORD commands that you should *"Defend the cause of the weak and fatherless; maintain the rights of the poor and oppressed. Rescue the weak and needy; deliver them from the hand of the wicked"* (Psalm 82:3-4).

Your Attitude Towards Your Enemies

The supreme example of the attitude to maintain towards one's enemies is demonstrated by the Almighty God. Though we were hostile towards Him and living in total violation of His established principles, He took the initiative to reconcile us to Himself through the cruel death of His only begotten Son on the cross of Calvary.

"But God demonstrates his own love for us in this: While we were still sinners, Christ died for us... For if, when we were God's enemies, we were reconciled to him through the death of his Son, how much more, having been reconciled, shall we be saved through his life!" (Romans 5:8,10).

"All this is from God, who reconciled us to himself through Christ and gave us the ministry of reconciliation: that God was reconciling the world to himself in Christ, not counting men's sins against them. And he has committed to us the message of reconciliation" (2 Corinthians 5:18-19).

We were sinners but Christ died for us!
We were God's enemies but He reconciled us to Himself!
He did not count our sins against us.
What, therefore, should be your attitude towards your enemies?

1. Love Your Enemies

"But I tell you who hear me: Love your enemies, do good to those who hate you" (Luke 6:27).

The Lord Jesus Christ asked us to maintain an attitude of love towards our enemies. This is an attitude that demonstrates maturity. The Greek word used here for love is the same used by the Lord in commanding us in Luke 10:27 to *"Love the Lord your God..."* So you are expected to love your enemies with the same kind of love with which you love God. Only that in God's case you have to do it will *"all your heart and with all your soul and all your strength and with all your mind"*.

It is the same word the Lord Jesus used to describe the Father's love for Him (John 10:17) and His love for the Father (John 14:31).

He used it to describe the Fathers love for the disciples and His own love for the disciples (John 14:21,23). He also used it in the command given to the disciples to love each other (John 15:17). This love has its origin in God and is put in our hearts by the Holy Spirit. Allow the Holy Spirit to impart love for your enemies in your heart.

2. Pray For Your Enemies

"But I tell you: Love your enemies and pray for those who persecute you" (Matthew 5:44).

A man's persecutors are also his enemies yet the Lord is asking that you pray for them. What many of us do most of the time is pray against our enemies. The Lord says you should pray for them. Pray for God to have mercy and open their eyes. This will cause you to become mature and it also reflects how mature you are.

3. Do Good To Your Enemies

"But love your enemies, do good to them, and lend to them without expecting to get anything back. Then your reward will be great, and you will be sons of the Most High, because he is kind to the ungrateful and wicked" (Luke 6:35).

Lending to your enemies is an act of goodness.

The Bible also says, *"If your enemy is hungry, give him food to eat; if he is thirsty, give him water to drink"* (Proverbs 25:21).

Maturity is the capacity to feed your enemies and seek their welfare even when they are seeking your down fall.

Your Attitude Towards The Rebelious

This concerns mostly those in authority. Whether you are a parent, a boss, a church leader or whatever sphere of authority you exercise, you will always face opposition from people. There are people who the devil will use to make things really difficult for you. Some will be totally conscious and aware of what they are doing while others will be ignorant. Maturity means you treat those who rebel against your authority as though they did not. That is why Paul said to Timothy, *"Those*

who oppose him he must gently instruct, in the hope that God will grant them repentance leading them to a knowledge of the truth"
(2 Timothy 2:25).

You act towards or speak to the rebellious in the hope that God will bring them to repentance. Rebellion is one of the great traps of satan. And he has many caught in this trap, unable to free themselves. When you see your brother or your sister in a trap, what do you do? Do you kill him or her, or seek for means to set him/her free?

Any rebel has been entrapped.
The rebellious flock has been trapped!
The rebellious wife has been trapped!
The rebellious child has been trapped!
The rebellious subordinate has been trapped!

Maturity means you doing all in your capacity to bring them to their senses and set them free from this great trap.

You can correct a rebellious person without being resentful or reactive. That is why the Bible says you should gently correct such.

Your Attitude Towards Rebuke And Correction

Infants take offense when they are rebuked or corrected. They see it as lack of love or humiliation. Some would even take it as a confrontation. Mature people rejoice when they are rebuked or corrected. They know it is for their own good. Mature people accept rebuke and correction without taking offense, no matter how painful the rebuke, correction, or discipline may be.

One mark of maturity is prudence. And the Bible says in Proverbs 15:5, *"Whoever heeds correction shows prudence."* So your degree of maturity is reflected by how much correction you are willing to accept. The Baby also says, *"Whoever heeds correction gains understanding"* (Proverbs 15:32). Understanding of the puzzles of life and the ways of God will cause you to become mature. There are people who tend to hate or resent those who rebuke and correct them. The Bible calls such mockers. And mockers are the most immature. The wise man loves and cherishes those who rebuke him. And wisdom is a sign of maturity (Proverbs 9:7-8).

CHAPTER 10

YOUR MATURITY IS DETERMINED BY, AND REFLECTED IN, YOUR TEACHABILITY

By *teachability*, I mean the disposition to learn, be taught, corrected, instructed, and rebuked without any inward or outward reaction. It is the disposition which says, *"I don't know all yet, I am willing to learn from some other person."*

You Don't Know Everything

Some people think they are an embodiment of wisdom and knowledge. They know everything perfectly such that they need no further knowledge. This portrays gross immaturity. Paul said. *"The man who thinks he knows something does not yet know as he ought to know"* (1 Corinthians 8:2).

If ever you think you know everything on a given subject, then you are deficient in knowledge. There is childish knowledge and there is mature knowledge. Childish knowledge is what causes people to become puffy because of what they know. *"Now about food sacrificed to idols: We know that we all possess knowledge. Knowledge puffs up, but love builds up"* (1 Corinthians 8:1).

You Can Be Teachable

> *"Instruct a wise man and he will be wiser still; teach a righteous man and he will add to his learning"* (Proverbs 9:9).

Wise people always make room to improve on their wisdom. They are open to learn from others. The mature are teachable. They are open to instruction. They want to learn and add to their learning. The immature think that they have arrived at the acme of knowledge.

Let's look at some examples in scripture:

1. Peter

> *"Bear in mind that our Lord's patience means salvation, just as our dear brother Paul also wrote you with the wisdom that God gave him. He writes the same way in all his letters, speaking in them of these matters. His letters contain some things that are hard to understand, which ignorant and unstable people distort, as they do the other Scriptures, to their own destruction"* (2 Peter 3:15-16).

Peter, that great Apostle, was writing about the letters of Paul. We see here that he did not claim to easily understand everything which Paul had written. In fact he acknowledged that they were hard to understand. By so doing, he was also acknowledging the special grace that was given Paul with respect to revelations. An immature person in Peter's position as the leader of The Twelve would have disputed some of the things Paul was saying. Besides he was not even among The Twelve. It was not so with Peter. He understood that about Paul it was said *"Then he said: 'The God of our fathers has chosen you to know his will and to see the Righteous One and to hear words from his mouth"* (Acts 22:14). This means Paul had access to some knowledge which was hidden from others, even from them (who were in Christ before Paul).

You must make room for the knowledge that God has given others. It is all by His sovereign choice. So things which you don't understand do not condemn except they are contrary to sound biblical doctrine.

Another example of Peter's maturity expressed through his teachability is seen, when they had backslidden and gone back to fishing. The LORD appeared to them after a toilsome night of fruitless fishing. When He gave the instruction as to where to drop the net, Peter's obedience brought about a miraculous catch. Now there was someone amongst them who was more discerning, because of his close contact with and love for the Lord. That was no other than the Apostle John.

> *"Then the disciple whom Jesus loved said to Peter, 'It is the Lord!' As soon as Simon Peter heard him say, 'It is the Lord,' he wrapped his outer garment around him (for he had taken it off) and jumped into the water"* (John 21:7).

Peter was not able to discern that it was the Lord who stood on the shore. But as soon as John mentioned it, he did not hesitate to learn from John. He did not say he was the leader and because he had not discerned it, it couldn't be so. Instead, as soon as he heard what John said, he acted on it. Do not let your pride and incapacity to be willing to learn from others, deprive you of your God-encounter and the blessing which follows.

Another aspect of *teachability* is the willingness to be led and the capacity to follow. Our glorious Lord said to Peter *"I tell you the truth, when you were younger you dressed yourself and went where you wanted; but when you are old you will stretch out your hands, and someone else will dress you and lead you where you do not want to go"* (John 21:18). The immature dress how they want, do what they want, go where they want and when they want. The mature are willing to be led and to follow. They voluntarily submit in rather trivial aspects. That is what *teachability* is all about.

2. Apollos

> *"Meanwhile a Jew named Apollos, a native of Alexandria, came to Ephesus. He was a learned man, with a thorough knowledge of the Scriptures. He had been instructed in the way of the Lord, and he spoke with great fervor and taught about Jesus accurately, though he knew only the baptism of John. He began to speak boldly in the*

synagogue. When Priscilla and Aquila heard him, they invited him to their home and explained to him the way of God more adequately. When Apollos wanted to go to Achaia, the brothers encouraged him and wrote to the disciples there to welcome him. On arriving, he was a great help to those who by grace had believed. For he vigorously refuted the Jews in public debate, proving from the Scriptures that Jesus was the Christ" (Acts 18:24-28).

The Bible lists the following qualities of Apollos:
- He was a learned man
- He had a thorough knowledge of the scriptures
- He had been instructed in the way of the Lord
- He spoke with great fervor
- He taught about Jesus accurately
- He spoke boldly in the synagogue

What qualities! But there was a handicap somewhere; he knew only the baptism of John. He had not yet been baptized into the Lord nor had he received the baptism of the Holy Ghost. Thus, his knowledge was not very adequate. That is why when Pricilla and Aquila heard him they invited him to their home and taught him the way of the Lord more adequately.

For Apollos to have accepted their invitation and be receptive of their teaching in spite of the above qualities of his, means that he was teachable. He knew that he did not know it all and was willing to learn from others. Some with such qualities, though with inadequate knowledge, would have, out of zeal, started their own school of ministry, thereby multiplying their inadequacies. This is what is creating confusion in the churches today. May God give us a spirit like the one Apollos had. One that is willing to learn. Can you for a moment take another look at the afore-mentioned qualities? If you were Apollos could you have accepted some other person to teach you?

Because Apollos was teachable, he learned all he could from Pricilla and Aquila and thereby made up for his inadequacies. That is why when he went to Achaia *"he was of great help to those who by grace had believed"*. He could vigorously refute the Jews in public debate, proving from the scriptures that Jesus was the Christ, thanks to his teachability.

Apollo's teachability *"caused him to mature so rapidly that he reached the status of an Apostle. He became very renowned in the church in Corinth. That is why some could say, 'I follow Paul'; another, 'I follow Apollos'; another, 'I follow Cephas'; still another, 'I follow Christ'"* (1 Corinthians 1:12). There is no height to which a person with a teachable heart can not rise. Every height is attainable in every sphere of life. What matters is not what you already know (for knowledge does expire), but rather what you are willing to know.

Some people will make unheard-of-progress, they will rise to untold heights if they would only humble themselves and become teachable.

Just the capacity to ask correct questions will help many develop their gifts and ministries, but this is what many lack today. You can improve on what you know. You can expand your horizon. You can extend your borders. You can rise to new heights just by being in possession of that virtue of teachability.

3. Nicodemus

See John 3:1-9

Some people are un-teachable because of their religious or social titles and positions. This was the situation of the Pharisees and teachers of the law. Their titles and position in society blinded them to the need to learn from the very One who was the embodiment of divine wisdom. Because they were used to being learned from, they did not want to learn from another or worst still be seen learning from another. What folly of the corrupt human heart!

Nicodemus was one of them and did not want to be seen learning from an *"unschooled Teacher"*, so he came at night. We thank God for his willingness to learn.

He began by acknowledging that Jesus was a teacher from God. He acknowledged the fact that God was with Jesus for he had seen the miraculous signs He performed. In his conversation with the Lord, Nicodemus was willing to ask questions. He did not pretend to know everything. Some of his questions sounded childish before the Master and so Jesus asked him, *"You are Israel's teacher, and do you not understand these things?"* (John 3:10). I am sure this one touched the ego of Nicodemus, however, fortunately he left enlightened. He acquired new knowledge which the others could never get. Above all, he left there born again. That is why when the rest of the counsel was speaking folly, he through his acquired knowledge spoke sense, and they took offence at him.

> *"Finally the temple guards went back to the chief priests and Pharisees, who asked them, "Why didn't you bring him in?" "No one ever spoke the way this man does," the guards declared. "You mean he has deceived you also?" the Pharisees retorted. "Has any of the rulers or of the Pharisees believed in him? No! But this mob that knows nothing of the law--there is a curse on them." Nicodemus, who had gone to Jesus earlier and who was one of their own number, asked, "Does our law condemn anyone without first hearing him to find out what he is doing?" They replied, "Are you from Galilee, too? Look into it, and you will find that a prophet does not come out of Galilee"* (John 7:45-52).

Many people will have to dissociate themselves from their current religious and social titles and positions so that they can become teachable. Those titles and positions are causing them to be proud and arrogant and therefore unable to learn and drink from the cup of others.

Because Nicodemus was teachable he was enlightened and became a disciple of the Lord Jesus, though in secret. That is why he had this great honour of burying the Lord Jesus Christ after His crucifixion (John 19:38-40).

CHAPTER 11

YOUR MATURITY IS DETERMINED BY, AND REFLECTED IN, YOUR UNDERSTANDING

Understanding is another great virtue which determines and also reflects the degree of maturity of everyone. People of great maturity are people of great understanding. The question you may ask is *"how can I measure my degree of understanding?"*. If you have asked yourself that question, then it is very appropriate. There are several ways in which understanding expresses itself and so by looking at these you will be able to measure your understanding.

Manifestations of Understanding

These are some of the ways through which understanding is expressed. I will not claim that the list is exhaustive.

The Ability to Shun Evil

"And he said to man, `The fear of the Lord--that is wisdom, and to shun evil is understanding" (Job 28:28).

The ability and willingness to say *"No"* to sin and all manner of evil is one way through which understanding is expressed. Some people expect others to *"understand"* with them by compromising to do evil. This is nothing but folly! Those who have understanding refuse to do evil, neither will they partake in it, no matter the apparent gain that may bring. What is your attitude towards sin? How do you react to *"opportunities"* to benefit from sinful compromise? If you have understanding you will persistently and resolutely say *"no"* to any offer of sin and compromise with the world.

Control of Your Speech

"A man who lacks judgment derides his neighbor, but a man of understanding holds his tongue" (Proverbs 11:12).

The capacity to keep one's tongue under control is another manifestation of understanding. The one who controls his tongue understands that words have power. They understand that a loose tongue has the power to cause untold damage and even destroy lives and ruin destinies. They understand that the damage caused by a single word might produce a wound which may need ten thousand words to heal. Only the immature, those who lack understanding underestimate the potentials of the tongue. James said, (James 3:5-8) you cannot tame the tongue, its only solution is to hold it back, that is, to put a tight rein on it.

Patience

"A patient man has great understanding, but a quick-tempered man displays folly" (Proverbs 14:29).

The ability to be patient is an expression of understanding. When you are patient with people, you express your understanding of their weakness and of the fact that we are still humans, in this body of clay, subject to failures and short comings. Patience is that virtue which causes you to make room for the weak and their weaknesses. It is what will cause you to endure pain and loss because you are seeking someone else's interest.

Integrity

"Folly delights a man who lacks judgment, but a man of understanding keeps a straight course" (Proverbs 15:21).

Corruption is one mark of the lack of judgment or understanding. Duplicity and crookedness in dealing with people and things is an expression of folly. One way in which understanding is expressed, is the capacity to be straightforward. Many people today are plagued by guile and dissimilitude. Falsehood and hypocrisy is the downfall of many. This just portrays a lack of understand. He who has understanding will be truthful, honest, and transparent to the core. People of understanding do not only shun evil but they keep away from every appearance of evil. They take a straight and transparent course even when they are misunderstood.

Good Life

"Who is wise and understanding among you? Let him show it by his good life, by deeds done in the humility that comes from wisdom" (James 3:13, emphasis mine).

Another way by which you can express your understanding is by your good life. Your life of service, giving, and helping others! Your life should portray the character of Christ and love for others.

Deeds Of Humility

"Who is wise and understanding among you? Let him show it by his good life, *by deeds done in the humility* that comes from wisdom." (James 3:13, emphasis mine)

There are deeds of humility. When you carry out deeds of service in humility you are expressing understanding of the divine principle of greatness. You are expressing understanding of the fact that we have to serve one another in love. You are expressing understanding of the fact that we have to consider others better than ourselves.

Knowing the Lord's Will

"Therefore do not be foolish, but understand what the Lord's will is" (Ephesians 5:17).
"For this reason, since the day we heard about you, we have not stopped praying for you and asking God to fill you with the knowledge of his will through all spiritual wisdom and understanding" (Colossians 1:9).

Another way you can become mature is by understanding the Lord's will. On the other hand understanding will grant you access into the will of God. Understanding leads you to understand the mind of the Father. God reveals His will to a man by granting him understanding of the things which please Him. Yeah, the things He takes delight in.

Knowledge of Christ

> *"My purpose is that they may be encouraged in heart and united in love, so that they may have the full riches of complete understanding, in order that they may know the mystery of God, namely, Christ"* (Colossians 2:2).
>
> *"The fear of the LORD is the beginning of wisdom, and knowledge of the Holy One is understanding"* (Proverbs 9:10).

When you explore the riches of understanding, you tap from the mysteries of God and receive revelation knowledge of Christ. As you know Christ your understanding increases.

CHAPTER 12

YOUR MATURITY IS DETERMINED BY, AND REFLECTED IN, YOUR RESPONSIBILITY

Your degree of maturity is greatly reflected by the extent to which you are responsible in doing what you are convinced God has called you to do. The LORD God never called anyone to be idle or to have nothing for which he or she is answerable.

There is something God made you and assigned you to be answerable for whether temporarily or permanently. There is confusion and conflict in many a congregation today because people have not understood their responsibilities as part of the body. It was exactly the situation of the church in Jerusalem, until the apostles began assuming some responsibility in the household of God.

"In those days when the number of disciples was increasing, the Grecian Jews among them complained against the Hebraic Jews because their widows were being overlooked in the daily distribution of food. So the Twelve gathered all the disciples together and said, "It would not be right for us to neglect the ministry of the word of God in order to wait on tables. Brothers, choose seven men from among you who are known to be full of the Spirit and wisdom. We will turn this responsibility over to them and will give our attention to prayer and the ministry of the word" (Acts 6:1-4).

Just as it is gross irresponsibility to have nothing doing in the household of God, it is equally irresponsible to attempt to do everything. The Apostles saw this truth and so decided to resolve the crisis at hand by deciding to relinquish some of their functions in order that they may fully concentrate on their *"major function"*.

It is not how many things you are in charge of that makes you responsible but whether you are in charge for that which God has equipped you, and given you grace, to do. When people do the things for which they do not have the grace to do, the result is chaos.

If the eye would want to be in charge of taste, the whole body will be forced to suffer because it surely will never be able to determine the taste of pepper. What happens when pepper gets into the eyes? Are there not some who are suffering because they have tried to do the things they have not received grace for? No matter how strong the hand is, it can never become the mouth, tough it may assist in the process of eating, it can never swallow the food.

That is why the Bible says,

"Just as each of us has one body with many members, and these members do not all have the same function" (Romans 12:4).

"But in fact God has arranged the parts in the body, every one of them, just as he wanted them to be" (1 Corinthians 12:18).

If people should understand that it is God who determines how each part of the body should look like and the position and function it should carry, then strife and confusion would be completely wiped off, and healing would become our portion.

Having seen the need to be responsible, let us know the ways in which responsibility is manifested and later on we shall look at some examples.

Dependability

Every responsible person can be and should be dependable. Dependability is essential in evaluating how responsible someone is. In fact without being dependable you cannot qualify anybody as being responsible. That is, it does not depend on the number of things you are in charge of but the extent to which you can be counted upon as being in charge, without disappointment.

I have often seen people who are in charge of things but who can never be counted upon. They are eye servants. When your eye is on them, they get the job going but when you are away you can be sure that, the job won't be done the way it was to be done had you been there with them.

Let us get an illustration of this from the Bible:

"Who then is the faithful and wise servant, whom the master has put in charge of the servants in his household to give them their food at the proper time? It will be good for that servant whose master finds him doing so when he returns. I tell you the truth, he will put him in charge of all his possessions. But suppose that servant is wicked and says to himself, 'My master is staying away a long time,' and he then begins to beat his fellow servants and to eat and drink with drunkards. The master of that servant will come on a day when he does not expect him and at an hour he is not aware of. He will cut him to pieces and assign him a place with the hypocrites, where there will be weeping and gnashing of teeth." (Matthew 24:45-51)

Faithfulness in this passage refers to the ability to be counted on for the performance of duty. This servant was *"in charge"* of the servants of a household. He was suppose to give food to his fellow servants at the proper time. Two things immediately emerge from here; the what and the when of responsibility. It is not only what to do which qualifies a responsibility but when to do it.

Responsibility means doing what you have to do when you have to do it, how you have to do it. We shall return to the *"when"* and *"how"* aspects later. Under dependability we will want to limit our discussion to the *"what"* aspect of it.

It is gross irresponsibility to do things only because of the presence of your superior and to neglect them when he is absent. This servant instead of giving food to his fellow servants as was expected of him, assumed the responsibility of a discipline master. Because he decided to become their discipline master, his responsibility of placing food within their reach was neglected. Of course when his master returned, it was not a question of whether he had done some other things but whether he had done what he was supposed to do. He was not given the responsibility to estimate how soon the master will return. When he assumed this function which was never given him, he put the whole household in disorder. Because the other servants could not eat at the proper time, they could not carry out their functions at the proper time. In addition to their hunger they received beatings from this self-appointed discipline master.

Are you doing that which your Master expects of you?

Are you doing that which He has called and equipped you for?

It is on that basis that your responsibility will be evaluated and not on whether you have kept yourself busy in His vine yard. How dependable are you? How committed are you in carrying out your function even when no one is there to ensure that you do it? Will you still do it and do it joyfully when the glory goes to another? That is what dependability is all about.

Discipline

Still referring to our passage in Matthew 24:45-51, we want to talk now on the *"when"* and the *"how"* of responsibility. Discipline is doing what you have to do, when you have to do it and how you have do it. And for this to happen, there must be some self-imposed constraints and restraints to enable you meet up with the *"when"* and *"how"* of your function. Before God, it is not only what you do that counts but when you do it and how you do it.

In the above passage the servant under discussion was not only expected to give his fellow servants food but to do so at the proper time. So there is a proper time for what God has equipped you for. That is why the Bible says, *"There is time for everything"* (Ecclesiastes 3:1a) and further says *"there is a proper time and procedure for every matter"* (Ecclesiastes 8:6a).

You see, the proper time is the *"when"* of a man's function and the proper procedure is the *"how"* aspect of it. Discipline is what will get you doing it when and how you are supposed to do it. You can measure how responsible you are and will become by measuring how disciplined you are. Do you concentrate and spend time on the non-essentials?

What are the boundary lines you have set for yourself which will give you signal that you are neglecting the *"when"* and *"how"* aspects of your responsibility. For, unless there are these clearly defined self-imposed constraints or boundary lines, you are bound to become an eye servant. And be sure that eye service has no place in the Kingdom. (Ephesians 6:5-6). The Master wants to put you in charge of His possessions (v 47) but He wants you to prove how dependable and how disciplined you are. That is, whether you are able to handle well, the *"what"*, *"when"*, and *"how"* aspects of your responsibility.

Diligence

How earnest you are in the execution of your duty also gives an indication of your degree of responsibility.

"And whatever you do, whether in word or deed, do it all in the name of the Lord Jesus, giving thanks to God the Father through him" (Colossians 3:17).

What does it mean to do all in the Name of the Lord? This means whatever duty you have you must do it as though the Lord Himself were benefiting from the service. See it as though the Lord Himself was right before you receiving the services you are performing.

Diligent Service Means Wholehearted Service

"Slaves, obey your earthly masters in everything; and do it, not only when their eye is on you and to win their favor, but with sincerity of heart and reverence for the Lord. Whatever you do, work at it with all your heart, as working for the Lord, not for men" (Colossians 3:22-23).

If you have a function, do it with all your heart and not with partial commitment. Partial commitment to the things of God brings no reward. That is why it must be with all your heart because God deserves your whole heart's commitment. You are to *"love the Lord your God with all your heart…"* therefore you are *"to serve Him with all your heart…"* (Deuteronomy 11:13)

Diligent Service Means Serving with all Your Might

"Whatever your hand finds to do, do it with all your might, for in the grave, where you are going, there is neither working nor planning nor knowledge nor wisdom" (Ecclesiastes 9:10).

Whatever responsibility you have, God wants you to do it with all your might. To be self-sparing in doing the things of God is to have missed out on the important issues of life. Your might represents the sum total of all your resources be it physical, material, financial, mental, emotional, intellectual or spiritual resources. You must bring all in your service of the Lord, leaving nothing behind. That is what it means to serve the Lord with all your might. All your faculties are to aid you in the performance of your duty.

Endless possibilities

God wants you to graduate from using your resources into using His, as you carry out your responsibility. But He will only promote you to this higher level of service when you have exhausted all your available resources. Peter said, *"If anyone speaks, they should do so as one who speaks the very words of God. If anyone serves, they should do so with the strength God provides, so that in all things God may be praised through Jesus Christ. To him be the glory and the power for ever and ever. Amen"* (1 Peter 4:11). But how can you serve with the LORD'S own strength when you have not put in your all? It is only by putting in your all that you gain access to that strength of the LORD.

Paul could say, *"To this end I labour, struggling with all his energy, which so powerfully works in me"* (Colossians 1:29) because he had given his all, so he had access to the supernatural energy of god available to those who put in their all without reservation. So you can measure your responsibility based on whether you have put in all you can and should in your service of the LORD.

Ability to Delegate

The ability to delegate is another manifestation of responsibility. Responsible people delegate authority and functions. Many people wear themselves out unnecessarily because they fail to delegate people to do things. They lack the capacity to trust anybody to do it well because they look at themselves with some kind of superiority. People who are afraid to delegate authority and functions do not have confidence in the people around them.

As we said in the beginning of this chapter, it is very irresponsible to attempt to do everything. The head, though involved in everything, cannot do everything. It plays only the role of coordinating the affairs of the body. If it should decide to become the legs, you can imagine the resulting disaster. It is a sign of immaturity when you try to do it all by yourself.

Learn it from Moses

You remember the scene in Exodus chapter eighteen when Jethro visited the Israelites while they were in the wilderness. He saw how Moses bore the whole responsibility of the people by himself and Jethro was deeply disturbed about it. He told Moses that, what he was doing was not wise because it was going to wear out not only him, but the people he was leading. Now listen to the counsel he gave to his son-in-law:

> "Moses' father-in-law replied, "What you are doing is not good. You and these people who come to you will only wear yourselves out. The work is too heavy for you; you cannot handle it alone. Listen now to me and I will give you some advice, and may God be with you. You must be the people's representative before God and bring their disputes to him. Teach them the decrees and laws and show them the way to live and the duties they are to perform. But select capable men from all the people--men who fear God, trustworthy men who hate dishonest gain--and appoint them as officials over thousands, hundreds, fifties and tens. Have them serve as judges for the people at all times but have them bring every difficult case to you; the simple cases they can decide themselves. That will make your load lighter, because they will share it with you. If you do this and God so commands, you will be able to stand the strain, and all these people will go home satisfied."

Moses listened to his father-in-law and did everything he said. He chose capable men from all Israel and made them leaders of the people, officials over thousands, hundreds, fifties and tens. They served as judges for the people at all times. The difficult cases they brought to Moses, but the simple ones they decided themselves. Then Moses sent his father-in-law on his way, and Jethro returned to his own country" (Exodus 18:17-27).

Thus in delegating responsibility:

1. **You must demonstrate:**
"Teach them... show them..."
2. **You must appoint:**
"Select capable men... and appoint them..."
3. **You must respect the judgements of your delegates:**
"Have them serve as judges... the simple cases they are to decide themselves..."
4. **You must define the extent of the functions and power of your delegates:**
"... but have them bring every difficult case to you; the simple cases they can decide themselves..."

Availability

Another way to evaluate how responsible you are is to measure how available you are. Responsible parents make themselves available to their children especially when they need them.

Availability means you are there *"at the service"* of the one who has delegated you. You ensure that they do not have to look for you or wait for you when you are needed.

"Suppose one of you had a servant plowing or looking after the sheep. Would he say to the servant when he comes in from the field, `Come along now and sit down to eat'? Would he not rather say, `Prepare my supper, get yourself ready and wait on me while I eat and drink; after that you may eat and drink'? Would he thank the servant because he did what he was told to do? So you also, when

you have done everything you were told to do, should say, 'We are unworthy servants; we have only done our duty'" (Luke 17:7-10).

Availability means you are there when your master wants you. You are also there to get *"yourself ready and wait"* on your master. You anticipate when he will need what and you make it available. That is what availability is all about. There are some people who are always around but are not available because they are not willing to get themselves ready to do what is expected of them. It is the willingness and the readiness, not just the presence that makes for availability. That is, it is how willing you are to do a thing and how ready you are for that thing that qualifies you as being available, not just your presence.

Accountability

Another measuring rod for responsibility and consequently maturity is accountability. Irresponsible people are not accountable to anybody nor do they want to be. To know how responsible a man or woman is, just check how accountable the person is and to whom. I just finished reading the book, *"Fire in his Bones"* about the late Arch Bishop Benson Idahosa. I was very impressed by his degree of accountability. As his ministry developed, he increasingly sought to be under authority and God was faithful, in response to his heart's desire and prayer, to lead him to the elderly Br. Elton. To him, the man of God ensured he rendered accounts on a monthly basis. No matter how busy his schedule was, he ensured that his meeting with brother Elton was not missed. He also became accountable to people like the Lindsays, especially to Mrs Lindsay even after the death of her husband. He never allowed his masculine ego to keep him from being accountable to a woman. I also read, sometime ago, how Watchman Nee was also accountable to an elderly lady.

It is not just whether a person is accountable that matters but to whom the person is accountable. You must be accountable to people who are more mature than you spiritually. Those who can rebuke, correct, teach and train you. Those who can tell you stop and you do so without any hesitation. Some people deceive themselves by gathering around them those who never rebuke or correct them. They are just building a gallows for themselves. If there is nobody who can tell you *"go"* and you *"go"* and *"stop"* and you *"stop"*, you are to be pitied among all men.

The apostle Paul, in spite of the fact that he was called and sent by the Lord Jesus Christ, made himself accountable to the other apostles who were in Christ before him. Time and time again he would visit them to render account of what he was doing.

These verses below show how accountable Paul was:-

"The whole assembly became silent as they listened to Barnabas and Paul telling about the miraculous signs and wonders God had done among the Gentiles through them" (Acts 15:12).

"When we arrived at Jerusalem, the brothers received us warmly. The next day Paul and the rest of us went to see James, and all the elders were present. Paul greeted them and reported in detail what God had done among the Gentiles through his ministry" (Acts 21:17-19).

"Then after three years, I went up to Jerusalem to get acquainted with Peter and stayed with him fifteen days" (Galatians 1:18).

"Fourteen years later I went up again to Jerusalem, this time with Barnabas. I took Titus along also. I went in response to a revelation and set before them the gospel that I preach among the Gentiles. But I did this privately to those who seemed to be leaders, for fear that I was running or had run my race in vain" (Galatians 2:1-2).

Foresight

Your responsibility is also reflected in and determined by your degree of foresight. By foresight I mean the ability to anticipate needs of the future and plan accordingly. The Bible says, *"But a noble man makes noble plans, and by noble deeds and stands"* (Isaiah 32:8). Of all the noble qualities of the wife of noble character, the foremost is foresight. She could anticipate needs and plan in advance.

Responsible people do not wait until they are confronted with the unforeseen. They anticipate and make provisions for the unseen. To leave things in the hands of chance is a sign of irresponsibility. I have come to discover that great men of faith and the anointing of the Holy Ghost are also men of foresight and noble planning.

Do you remember the parable of the ten virgins?
(see Matthew 25:1-13)

What was the difference between the wise ones and the foolish ones? The only difference was foresight. Five had foresight which the others lacked. Their foresight caused them to anticipate the need for extra oil and so made provision for it. The others waited until the need for extra oil arose. Why were they disqualified by the bridegroom? Because their lack of foresight was a sign of irresponsibility and no responsible man would want to get married to a woman who cannot plan. Foresight leads to planning which is a sign of maturity.

You Can Be Responsible

There are many things for which you can become responsible in the household of God. You were never meant to be *"a do-nothing-always-there-spectator"*. Look for something, no matter how mean you consider it and take charge of, so that you are held responsible when anything is lacking in that domain. You can ask your pastor or group leader to assign you a responsibility.

These examples can help you:

"But the four principal gatekeepers, who were Levites, were entrusted with the responsibility for the rooms and treasuries in the house of God. They would spend the night stationed around the house of God, because they had to guard it; and they had charge of the key for opening it each morning" (1 Chronicles 9:26-27).

- You can become a gatekeeper, spiritually guarding the gates of your church by your prayers and intercession.

"A Levite named Mattithiah, the firstborn son of Shallum the Korahite, was entrusted with the responsibility for baking the offering bread. Some of their Kohathite brothers were in charge of preparing for every Sabbath the bread set out on the table. Those

who were musicians, heads of Levite families, stayed in the rooms of the temple and were exempt from other duties because they were responsible for the work day and night" (1 Chronicles 9:31-33).
- You can train yourself to play a particular musical instrument and take charge of it.
- You can clean the rooms in your church.

"The priests, who were heads of families, numbered 1,760. They were able men, responsible for ministering in the house of God" (1 Chronicles 9:13).

"Shallum son of Kore, the son of Ebiasaph, the son of Korah, and his fellow gatekeepers from his family (the Korahites) were responsible for guarding the thresholds of the Tent[n] just as their fathers had been responsible for guarding the entrance to the dwelling of the LORD" (1 Chronicles 9:19).

"The LORD said to Aaron, "You, your sons and your father's family are to bear the responsibility for offenses against the sanctuary, and you and your sons alone are to bear the responsibility for offenses against the priesthood" (Numbers 18:1).

"It is the Levites who are to do the work at the Tent of Meeting and bear the responsibility for offenses against it. This is a lasting ordinance for the generations to come. They will receive no inheritance among the Israelites" (Numbers 18:23).

CHAPTER 13

YOUR MATURITY IS DETERMINED BY, AND REFLECTED IN, YOUR INITIATIVE

Another gage for maturity is initiative; the capacity to intrinsically do things for the benefit of others. It is very closely related to responsibility. However, not every responsible person has good initiative. There are people who must always be told what to do. This does not make them irresponsible as all the qualities of responsibility can be seen in that which they have been assigned to do, though the motivation was external. Let us look at different ways in which initiative can be manifested:

Hospitality

> "Abraham looked up and saw three men standing nearby. When he saw them, he hurried from the entrance of his tent to meet them and bowed low to the ground. He said, "If I have found favor in your eyes, my lord, do not pass your servant by. Let a little water be brought, and then you may all wash your feet and rest under this tree. Let me get you something to eat, so you can be refreshed and then go on your way--now that you have come to your servant."
> "Very well," they answered, "do as you say." (Genesis 18:2-5)

Your degree of maturity is determined by, and reflected in, your initiative in offering hospitality. Hospitality is that virtue that pushes you to make room for others within your resources. It is different from generosity in that it necessitates a close contact and might necessitate a little inconvenience for the one offering the hospitality.

- Offering them water to watch their feet
- Offering them a place of rest
- Offering them something to eat.

If you ever think, these were but ordinary services then think of what the Lord Jesus said to the Pharisee who had invited Him for dinner: *"Then he turned toward the woman and said to Simon, "Do you see this woman? I came into your house. You did not give me any water for my feet, but she wet my feet with her tears and wiped them with her hair. You did not give me a kiss, but this woman, from the time I entered, has not stopped kissing my feet. You did not put oil on my head, but she has poured perfume on my feet"* (Luke 7:44-46).

This Pharisee was generous enough to invite Jesus for dinner (v 36) but the comment above, by the Lord shows that, though he was generous, he lacked the initiative to be hospitable. Your initiative for hospitality reflects how mature you are.

Helping Others

"Before he had finished praying, Rebekah came out with her jar on her shoulder. She was the daughter of Bethuel son of Milcah, who was the wife of Abraham's brother Nahor. The girl was very beautiful, a virgin; no man had ever lain with her. She went down to the spring, filled her jar and came up again.

The servant hurried to meet her and said, "Please give me a little water from your jar."

"Drink, my lord," she said, and quickly lowered the jar to her hands and gave him a drink. After she had given him a drink, she said, "I'll draw water for your camels too, until they have finished drinking." So she quickly emptied her jar into the trough, ran back to the well to draw more water, and drew enough for all his camels. Without saying a word, the man watched her closely to learn whether or not the LORD had made his journey successful" (Genesis 24:15-21).

Abraham had decided to get a wife for his forty-year-old son, Isaac, and so he sent his chief servant on this mission (to get a wife amongst his relatives). After a very long journey he arrived his destination but decided to rest outside the town. He decided to determine the wife for his master's son by playing a test of maturity, through the girls' initiative to help others. Many young men and women have woefully failed some tests because of this lack of initiative to help others.

In the above passage, Rebecca demonstrated her maturity through her initiative. She decided to help even beyond what she had been asked to do. The Bible says *"she quickly… ran back…"* (v 20). People with the initiative to help others do so with zeal and enthusiasm. They are not reluctant because it is not as though they were acting out of external pressure to do what they would otherwise not want to do.

You see, even if Rebecca had stopped at just offering the man a drink, she would have been very generous in sacrificing both her time and energy. However she would have failed to demonstrate her initiative to help, which is what the man was looking for. Her beauty and hard work could not have demonstrated what he was looking for in a woman worthy to be the wife of his master's son.

It couldn't have been enough to just respond to the man's request for help. Any normal, balanced, socially fit person will offer water to a thirsty man. The difference here is that by offering water to his camels Rebecca demonstrated her discretion to know that, if the man was thirsty, then the camels on which he and his luggage mounted should be of greater need.

There is someone watching to see your initiative to help beyond just a response.

Meeting Needs

"When Moses finished setting up the tabernacle, he anointed it and consecrated it and all its furnishings. He also anointed and consecrated the altar and all its utensils. Then the leaders of Israel, the heads of families who were the tribal leaders in charge of those who were counted, made offerings. They brought as their gifts before the LORD six covered carts and twelve oxen--an ox from each leader and a cart from every two. These they presented before the tabernacle" (Numbers 7:1-4).

These leaders took the initiative to make offerings so as to provide for the tabernacle. After Moses had finished setting up the tabernacle, he anointed it and set it apart. They saw the need to facilitate the work in the

Tent of meeting. It should be noted that they were not responding to any request. It was all on their own initiative that they anticipated the needs and decide to make an offering in that respect. The fact that God had to instruct Moses to accept the offering from them, telling him how they were to be used, indicates that it was not a command they were obeying (V5). People with initiative do not only wait until they receive a command.

What about David? He took the initiative to provide a resting (dwelling) place for the Ark of the Covenant when he built a tent for it and desired to build a temple for the Lord. Though the Lord did not allow him to build the temple, he had the singular privilege to receive from the Lord the detailed design of how the temple was going to look like, the different materials to be used etc. Also David provided from his personal treasury most of the gold, silver, and bronze that were used in the construction of the temple.

Your maturity is determined by, and reflected in, your initiative to anticipate needs and provide for those needs even when there is no personal interest or benefit. Today, churches are in great need of people with this kind of initiative; meeting the needs in the household of God. They do not wait until appeals are launched. While others are waiting for appeals, they go about looking for the needs they can meet and actually meet them.

Peacemaking

The human environment is most of the time plagued with conflicts of diverse sorts; from simple misunderstandings to open strife and discord. Every society needs people who demonstrate maturity through their peacemaking initiatives. Where this is lacking, simple misunderstandings may aggravate into active animosity and open hatred. Let us look at examples where someone demonstrated her maturity through her peacemaking initiative:

Abigail (see 1 Samuel 25)

Abigail was the wife of Nabal, a stingy, surly, and mean Calebite (Descendant of Caleb). When David was on exile, he had protected this man's sheep and shepherds from raiding bands in the desert, all the while they were with him. It was sheep shearing time and David thought it wise to make a demand on Nabal which he felt was normal. But Nabal resorted to insulting the men David had sent. He prepared himself for an all-out attack on Nabal and his household. Now when the news of her husband's misbehavior reached the ears of Abigail, the Bible says she took the initiative to pacify David (1 Samuel 25:18-28).

Her actions above demonstrated her maturity in handling conflict. She took all the necessary steps on her own initiative to appease David and his men. This prevented a catastrophe not only for her family and household but for the whole kingdom of Israel by preventing their future king from shedding blood because of revenge.

Joab (see 2 Samuel 14)

Joab also demonstrated his peacemaking initiative when he sought to reconcile the king with his estranged son Absalom. Absalom had murdered his brother Amnon and escaped to the king of Geshur. Joab noticed that the king actually longed for his son and so he decided to work out a reconciliation plan which worked and brought about Absalom's return to Jerusalem. The fact that he went off-hand is a totally different story.

If you must become mature in whatever domain of life, you're to take initiatives toward making and sustaining peace in your environment; whether it be at work, at school, in the neighborhood, or in the family.

Do you remember the wise woman at Abel Beth Maacah? When Sheba raised trouble against David he went and sought refuge in that city (see 2 Samuel 20). Joab and his army kept pursuit of him and besieged the city. They began battering the wall to bring it down when a wise woman inside the city took the initiative to make peace so as to save her city from the eminent rampage.

In order to maintain their legacy as the *"peaceful and faithful in Israel"* she had to go about and advise the people of that city to do away with Sheba so the siege could end. And for sure, her initiative brought about the withdrawal of the troops and thus the city was saved. Had she not taken the initiative towards peacemaking, her own life and the true destiny of the whole city would have been destroyed.

Risk Taking

Many people have their lives at a standstill because of lack of initiative to take risks. Your stalemate may owe to the lack of risk-taking initiatives. A life without risk appears safe but it will be stunted and lopsided in several aspects. In fact you can not serve and accomplish God's purpose for your life without this risk-taking initiative. It is imperative and indispensable for progress whether in business, ministry, academics or any other aspect.

Those who have grown to maturity are those who have taken the highest risks. Risk-taking gives you a world of experience that others who are afraid to take such risks will never have.

David's maturity was enhanced as he took risks at different times as the need arose:

- He chased and killed a bear
- He chased and killed a lion
- He confronted and defeated Goliath

Each risk he took, gave him some degree of maturity to take a greater risk.

What about Jonathan, Saul's son? The whole Israelite army, in fear of the Philistines, had gone into hiding in caves. Some had even defected to the Philistines (see Isaiah 14). However, Jonathan took the risk to confront the Philistines and this brought about a victory for the whole Israeli army.

Your life may still be in some kind of unnecessary confine and bondage because you have refused to take a little risk-bearing initiative. The man who bears risk has no limit, no obstacle he cannot surmount, no barrier he cannot bring down, no failure he cannot confront. There is no height to which such a person cannot not rise. May you become a man, woman, boy, or girl of initiative:

- In hospitality
- In helping others
- In meeting needs
- In peacemaking
- and in risk-taking.

CHAPTER 14

OUR MATURITY IS DETERMINED BY, AND REFLECTED IN, YOUR CAPACITY TO TRUST

Your degree of trust reflects your degree of maturity and your capacity to trust determines how mature you become. Nowadays many people trust in different things. Some trust in their money, some in their social status, other in their appearance, tribe, race, background and the like. But for the child of God, trust can't be placed in any of such things. We have a different set of things to put our trust in. And these we are going to look at in this Chapter and see also the benefits of trust.

What then should you put your trust in?

Trust In The Lord

"Trust in the LORD with all your heart..." (Proverbs 3:5a)

What doest it mean to trust in the Lord?

The Hebrew Word used in this verse is bâtach which means to take refuge, to be confident, to be bold, to be sure and to hope in. This means in everything you do, you are confident in the Lord. You are sure that God is in control. You face life knowing that God is your refuge from all harm. So you live carefree, void of every manner of anxiety or worry. You are sure that God's purposes stand forever and that He has you under His watchful eye.

It also means God becomes your reference and standard in everything you think, say or do. You trust Him by surrendering totally to His leadership, knowing that He has the best in store for you. When He commands, you quickly obey because you are confident that He has the best plan, knows the best way, and understands the best time for everything. In a nutshell, trusting in the Lord is submitting to His sovereign will with tranquility.

Trust In His Name

"Some trust in chariots and some in horses, but we trust in the name of the LORD our God." (Psalm 20:7)

"In him our hearts rejoice, for we trust in his holy name." (Psalm 33:21)

The Lord has given us His Name as our access to the Father. That Name gives us access into all that the Father has. Through the Name of Jesus we can reach into God's storehouse and claim our needs through the gracious provision of the Father. The Name has been given us as protection, as a means of salvation, healing and deliverance. The Name will work for you in the degree to which you trust the Name. That Name Jesus, is a wonderful Name to which every knee must bow. In fact, all things visible and invisible, pay obeisance to that Name.

Your degree of trust in that Name reflects how mature you are. The mature understand that, Jesus' Name carries with it divine power for breakthrough when it is mentioned by those who trust in the It. Also your trust in that Name will determine your maturity. If you lack trust in that Name, you will remain a Lilliput and make no progress in this path of godliness.

Trust In His Word

"Then I will answer the one who taunts me, for I trust in your word" (Psalm 119:42).

When you trust in God's Word you trust in the precepts and principles which govern the universe. Trust in the word of God gives you a ready answer to every assault from the enemy. When you trust in the

Word your whole life becomes built on the word. You store it in your heart. You believe all that God has said in His word and nothing moves your confidence. When you trust in the Word you understand that God will always do what He says He will, when He wills and how He wills. You make your requests based on the word and you are confident that they will be granted. You choose to believe what the word says in spite of circumstances pointing or declaring the contrary. The word becomes your measuring rod and everything is judged, approved or disapproved on the basis of what the Word of God says in spite of how one feels.

Trust In the Light

"Put your trust in the light while you have it, so that you may become sons of light." When he had finished speaking, Jesus left and hid himself from them" (John 12:36).

The Lord Jesus Christ told the Jews to put their trust in the light. Who is the light? Some time earlier He had declared: "When Jesus spoke again to the people, he said, "I am the light of the world. Whoever follows me will never walk in darkness, but will have the light of life" (John 8:12).

"While I am in the world, I am the light of the world" (John 9:5).

For you to escape the dark places of this life you must put your trust in Jesus. That is why He said. *"Trust in God; trust also in Me"* (John 14:1b). As you trust in the light your path becomes brighter with each passing day. You refuse to move in any direction to which the light has not yet shone. Your steps are directed and dictated by the light. And you are confident that the light will lead you to your God-ordained destiny.

Trust In His Love

"But I trust in your unfailing love; my heart rejoices in your salvation" (Psalm 13:5).

When you trust in God's love you believe that His love is too strong for you to break yourself from it. You know that it is too high that you can't get over even if you wanted to; so wide that you can't get out of, even when you stray; so deep that you can't get under even when you fall. Like the Apostle Paul, you can confidently ask, *"Who shall separate us from the love of Christ? Shall trouble or hardship or persecution or famine or nakedness or danger or sword?"* (Romans 8:35) and in the same breathe respond that, *"No, in all these things we are more than conquerors through him who loved us. For I am convinced that neither death nor life, neither angels nor demons, neither the present nor the future, nor any powers, neither height nor depth, nor anything else in all creation, will be able to separate us from the love of God that is in Christ Jesus our Lord"* (Romans 8:37-39).

What Trust Will Do for You

There are certain experiences you enter into only as you grow in your capacity to trust in the Lord; in His Word, in His Name, In His love, and in the Light.

It Will Bring You Deliverance

"In you our fathers put their trust; they trusted and you delivered them" (Psalm 22:4).

Heaven has decided that no one who trusts in the Lord should be in any kind of bondage. Those who trust enter into freedom in places where even the mighty could be kept bound. I don't know in which area in life you need deliverance. If you will just trust in the Lord and in Him only, He will demonstrate His infinite power to bring about your deliverance from whatever seeks to keep you bound.

It Will Ensure That You Are Not Disappointed

"They cried to you and were saved; in you they trusted and were not disappointed" (Psalm 22:5).

Many people nowadays are getting disappointed in many things. The systems of the world which in times past use to prove reliable are increasingly breaking millions of hearts today.

Those who trust in the Lord have nothing to fear. Because God never fails those who trust in Him. He always proves Himself Lord whenever you trust Him.

Bible History has several testimonies of those who have trusted the Lord in seemingly bizarre circumstances and were never disappointed. Christian biography has thousands of such testimonies documented. As you read such biography you too become inspired and motivated to put your complete trust in the One who never fails nor disappoints.

It Will Separate You from Vanity

"I hate those who cling to worthless idols; I trust in the LORD"
(Psalm 31:6).

Many people are just vain, they cling to worthless things because they lack trust in God. No one can trust in the Lord and be vain at the same time. There is something about trust in God that drives away vanity and frees a man from the vain mind set. Many are in a mad pursuit for the wrong things because they have not put their trust in God. They cling to idols because they think those idols (be it riches, fame, possessions, relationships, profession etc) will provide them with what they can only find in God. When you trust in the Lord, your values change from vanity to things which are eternal. You ensure that you are totally free from any form of idolatry by giving God the first place in all things.

It Will Boost Your Confidence

"For I hear the slander of many; there is terror on every side; they conspire against me and plot to take my life. But I trust in you, O LORD; I say, 'You are my God'" (Psalm 31:13-14).

"When I am afraid, I will trust in you. In God, whose word I praise, in God I trust; I will not be afraid. What can mortal man do to me?" (Psalm 56:3-4)

In the face of pressure, slander, false accusations, oppositions and all manner of conspiracy, what will keep your head high is your trust in God. When you trust in the Lord you keep going through things and places where others have given up. You keep standing in the very places where others have woefully fallen.

David found himself surrounded by those who sought his life but his trust in the Lord gave him an unwavering confidence such that he could brave it through all of that.

Do you want to brave it through any and every circumstance in life? Put your complete and total trust absolutely in God alone. This will render you invincible in the face of trails.

It Will Enhance Your Capacity to Do Good

"Trust in the LORD and do good; dwell in the land and enjoy safe pasture" (Psalm 37:3).

When you trust in the Lord you will always find yourself doing good to all those around you, even to those who are undeserving. You adopt a *"for God's sake"* attitude in all you do. You will not hesitate to sacrifice anything for someone because you trust in the Word which says you should do good and expect no return from it.

Have you ever wondered why some people find such joy in doing good even to those who actively seek their ruin? Their secret is in the fact that they trust in the Lord and therefore acts of goodness flow *"naturally"* to others. It is as if trust in the Lord generates a river of life-refreshing water from them that flows continuously to others. Your capacity to do good will be greatly enhanced when you trust the Lord.

It Will Brighten Your Life

"Commit your way to the LORD; trust in him and he will do this: He will make your righteousness shine like the dawn, the justice of your cause like the noonday sun" (Psalm 37:5-6).

When you trust in the Lord He will make your righteousness to shine like the dawn. Everything around you will be affected by the brightness of your righteous life. Your spiritual ambiance will be like the sun at its peak of brightness. And this brightness will dispel darkness wherever you step your feet. In fact darkness will have no other option but to flee from the brightness of your light.

Have you noticed that there are people in whose presence darkness does not stand? The secret is that they have put their complete trust in God. You too can grow into that, if only you trust completely in the Lord.

It Makes You Blessed

"Blessed is the man who makes the LORD his trust, who does not look to the proud, to those who turn aside to false gods" (Psalm 40:4).

It is such a blessed thing to trust in the Lord. He who places all His trust in the Lord enters into a realm of the blessed life that others will never enter. Trust, absolute trust in the Lord for all your needs known and unknown is an open door to the blessed kind of life.

Think of all the elements that constitute the life of a blessed man. Trust in God gives you the key into every realm of blessing and you can access, God's storehouse any time and retrieve the richest of blessing as the need arises. Ask anyone who is living a blessed life, the secret of this blessedness and he will tell you, absolute trust in God! Without it you cannot access the realm of the fullness of blessing.

What is depriving you of the blessed life is that thing you have placed your trust apart from God. It is that thing or person or system your heart always turns to when an emergency arises. Until you come to the place where you turn to the left and see only God, turn to the right and see only God, even when you look behind you see only God, then the blessed life is far from you.

Mature people have entered into the blessedness of this kind of life because God has become their All in all. They have no other place to run to but God. No other thing to look up to but God. No-one else to turn to but God. They have come to realize that unless God acts in their favor they are finished. And so they live confidently in the place where all has been handed over into the hands of the God in whom they trust.

It Will Make You Flourish in God's House

"But I am like an olive tree flourishing in the house of God; I trust in God's unfailing love for ever and ever" (Psalm 52:8).

This signifies fruitfulness in your God-ordained ministry. Trust in the Lord will cause you to produce abundant fruits in the domain of your service. You will ever be fresh when others are growing dry. You become a channel of the anointing.

It Will Give You Unshakable Stamina

"Those who trust in the LORD are like Mount Zion, which cannot be shaken but endures forever" (Psalm 125:1).

When you trust in the Lord you become like Mount Zion which cannot be shaken. Trust gives a stamina which no storm of life can shake. You become unmoved by circumstances, apparent failure or lack. Others look and wonder why all around you is shaking and quaking but you seem to maintain your composure. Why? Because trust causes you to spread your spiritual roots deep in the Lord until you are firmly established that nothing moves you. You laugh and mock at the rage of satan and his demons knowing that you are in a place where *"nothing moves and nothing harms"* you.

It Will Give Your Life Direction

"Let the morning bring me word of your unfailing love, for I have put my trust in you. Show me the way I should go, for to you I lift up my soul" (Psalm 143:8).

Those who have put their complete trust in God awaken expecting to hear from God. They watch for the morning with great expectation of what the Lord will tell them concerning their day. They are sure to receive direction from the Lord because they depend on Him for the power to choose rightly. They wait for the Lord's direction before they tread any path.

> *You remember the verse which says "your word is lamp to my feet and a light for my path"* (Psalm 119:105).

As the one who trusts in God's word reads it he sees where to place the next step in the right direction. That is why David prayed to the Lord *"Direct my footsteps according to Your word; let no sin rule over me"* (Psalm 119:133). As you trust in God's word your every footstep is directed by it because in it you will find very clear instructions and principles for life. As you trust in the word it gives you power and enhances your dominion over sin. Trust will give you direction.

It Will Provide Safe Escape from Trouble

> *"But I will rescue you on that day, declares the LORD; you will not be handed over to those you fear. I will save you; you will not fall by the sword but will escape with your life, because you trust in me, declares the LORD"* (Jeremiah 39:17-18).

When things are not going and there is danger on every side, God will provide you a safe escape from calamity. When you trust in the Lord, He takes special charge to keep you safe from all harm. God is bound to come to your rescue when you trust in Him.

When you trust in Him you will not be handed over to disease and sickness.

When you trust in Him you will not be handed over to the host of wickedness seeking your life or property. If they, by any means come near you it is so that through them God will grant you promotion as was the case of Job.

It Will Cause You to Enjoy God's Care

> *"The LORD is good, a refuge in times of trouble. He cares for those who trust in him"* (Nahum 1:7).

Our God is a God who cares for His creation and particularly for His children, but trust is what will give you and me access to enjoy this care.

Those who trust in the Lord understand that it is His will to have all their physical, emotional, mental, social and spiritual needs met. And so they cease from all care, worry or anxiety about their personal needs. Because of this they have access into the next benefit of trust.

It Will Cause You to Enter Rest

When you trust in the Lord you cease from every form of worry and anxiety, and by so doing you enter into rest. The Lord Jesus said, *"Do not let your hearts be troubled. Trust in God, trust also in Me"* (John 14:1). Thus when you trust in God and in His Christ, your heart is freed from all manner of trouble. It enters into a state of rest and tranquility.

Do you want to enter into a state of rest? Then you will have to trust the Lord.

It Opens the Way into a Life of Joy and Peace

"May the God of hope fill you with all joy and peace as you trust in him, so that you may overflow with hope by the power of the Holy Spirit" (Romans 15:13).

Trust is the nozzle that controls the flow of joy and peace. When you trust in the Lord, He fills you with joy and peace. Do you see that? He fills you! Not just a little joy or some measure of peace but He opens the tap until you are filled to the point of an overflow that contaminates those around you.

Trust is the key to a joyful and exuberant joy. What saps joy from the life of many people is their lack of trust. Trust is what discharges you of all burdens and lay them on the Lord. You become at peace and at ease in the midst of unrest and turmoil.

When Should You Trust?

1. When God Is Silent.

"I will wait for the LORD, who is hiding his face from the house of Jacob. I will put my trust in him" (Isaiah 8:17).

When God is silent and things seem not to move, it is still time to trust Him. Do not be one who seems to trust when God speaks but fail to trust when He is silent. Our God speaks even through His silence.

2. **When All Is Dark**

"Who among you fears the LORD and obeys the word of his servant? Let him who walks in the dark, who has no light, trust in the name of the LORD and rely on his God" (Isaiah 50:10).

When you feel engulfed by darkness with no light shining on the horizon, it is time to trust the Lord. No darkness is dark to Him. Trust and reliance on the Lord go hand in glove. Do not develop self-made schemes to provide yourself with light where God has not shone His light. The darkness can be an indication for you to halt and listen.

Trust at All Times

"Trust in him at all times, O people; pour out your hearts to him, for God is our refuge" (Psalm 62:8).

When things are fine, trust in Him

When things are "bad", trust in Him.

When you are strong, trust in Him.

When you are weak, trust in Him

When you are amply supplied, trust in Him.

When you are in need, trust in Him

When things are the way you want, trust in Him.

When things are going contrary to what you want, trust in God. Trust at all times!

CHAPTER 15

YOUR MATURITY IS DETERMINED BY, AND REFLECTED IN, YOUR CAPACITY TO YIELD

The capacity to yield refers to that disposition of surrendering to the will, leading, and demands of others against self-will.

It is very natural for somebody to do that which originates from himself. It is also very natural for someone to accept and joyfully following someone else's leading when it is in the direction of one's self will. However, it takes a high capacity to yield for anyone to do what is contrary to the desires of the natural man.

The ability to yield can be compared to white light which when split will give several different colors. The different colors are also light but will never produce the same effect, individually, as white light will produce. There are a number of aspects which together constitute the ability to yield. Now let us examine these different qualities. For a person to be yielded, we are looking for the presence or expression of all of these in the life of that individual.

Abandonment

The very first thing we are looking for in the life of a yielded individual is abandonment. By abandonment, I mean the giving up of selfish pursuits for the sole sake of the cross i.e. that which God has called a man to do. To better understand this, let us look at the man who came to Jesus. He was willing to follow Jesus but he lacked this element of abandonment which would have caused him to yield to the demands of the Master.

> *"He said to another man, "Follow me." But the man replied,*
> *"Lord, first let me go and bury my father."*
> *Jesus said to him, "Let the dead bury their own dead, but you go*
> *and proclaim the kingdom of God."*
> *Still another said, "I will follow you, Lord; but first let me go back*
> *and say good-by to my family."*
> *Jesus replied, "No one who puts his hand to the plow and looks*
> *back is fit for service in the kingdom of God"* (Luke 9:59-62).

Both of these guys in the passage above were willing to follow the Master but they lacked the element of abandonment. They had not given up everything that was behind them. What about the rich young ruler? He wanted eternal life but missed it all together because he could not abandon all for the sake of following the Master. Was he called? Yes; like our two friends above! But they did not respond or fulfill their calling because they lacked abandonment.

Peter told the Lord, *"We have left everything to follow You!"* (Mark 10:28). That is the testimony of abandonment. And was he speaking the truth? Yes, he was! The Bible says.

> *"When they had done so, they caught such a large number of fish*
> *that their nets began to break. So they signaled their partners in the*
> *other boat to come and help them, and they came and filled both*
> *boats so full that they began to sink. When Simon Peter saw this,*
> *he fell at Jesus' knees and said, "Go away from me, Lord; I am a*
> *sinful man!" For he and all his companions were astonished at the*
> *catch of fish they had taken, and so were James and John, the sons*
> *of Zebedee, Simon's partners. Then Jesus said to Simon, "Don't be*
> *afraid; from now on you will catch men." So they pulled their boats*
> *up on shore, left everything and followed him."* (Luke 5:6-11)

> *"After this, Jesus went out and saw a tax collector by the name of*
> *Levi sitting at his tax booth. "Follow me," Jesus said to him, and*
> *Levi got up, left everything and followed him."* (Luke 5:27-28)

In the first instance, Peter and his partners had just had a wonderful once-in-a-life time catch of fish yet in response to the call, they abandoned everything and followed Jesus. This is abandonment! In the second instance Mathew (Levi) abandoned his lucrative tax-collector position to become a follower of Jesus. The idea of abandonment here is to give up all that will hinder, and embrace all that will facilitate the fulfillment of your call.

Paul said, *"But whatever was to my profit I now consider loss for the sake of Christ. What is more, I consider everything a loss compared to the surpassing greatness of knowing Christ Jesus my Lord, for whose sake I have lost all things. I consider them rubbish, that I may gain Christ and be found in him, not having a righteousness of my own that comes from the law, but that which is through faith in Christ--the righteousness that comes from God and is by faith"* (Philippians 3:7-9).

He left everything that could hinder his calling and embraced everything that will enhance his calling, whether the things were *"good"* or *"bad"*.

Abandonment is a necessity for everyone who must grow into maturity. However, abandonment for you will be different from abandonment for me or for someone else but the bottom line is giving up everything that will hinder the call of God on a man's life. Now these things will be different because we all have different callings.

Willingness

Another component of a yielded nature is willingness. No one can be considered yielded if he or she does not maintain a willing disposition. The Psalmist cried out, *"I desire to do your will, O my God; Your law is within my heart"* (Psalm 40:8). It is this desire to do God's will, in the heart of a man that we refer to as willingness. When God asked, in the vision which Isaiah saw, *"who will go for us"*, Isaiah's response of *"Here am I send me"* expressed his willingness to be used of God. Willingness is an integral part of yielding.

Willingness Ushers You the Best

"If you are willing and obedience, you will eat the best from the land" (Isaiah 1:19).

When you are willing to do the will of God, when you are willing to be used of God wherever, however, whenever, and in whatever capacity, the best of the land of blessing will be within your reach. God wants and has programmed nothing for us but the best. It is this willingness that grants you access into the best. Willingness will bring about maturity. And you know that the best things are the mature ones.

The LORD Delights In Those Who Are Willing

"When the princes in Israel take the lead, when the people willingly offer themselves-- praise the LORD!" (Judges 5:2)
"My heart is with Israel's princes, with the willing volunteers among the people. Praise the LORD!" (Judges 5:9)

It is a sweet-smelling perfume unto the Lord when His people willingly offer themselves to His service. God says His heart is with the willing volunteers among His people. When God looks at His people, He looks for hearts that are willing and offers His heart to them in return. Will you not be pleased to have the heart of the King of the universe with you? Oh! Become willing and He will take delight in you.

Among those who served king Jehoshaphate, there was *"Amasiah son of Zicri, who volunteered himself for the service of the LORD with 200.000"* (2 Chronicles 17:16).

God wants those who will volunteer themselves by saying *"Here I am, I have come – it is written about me in the scroll. I desire to do Your will, O my God; Your law is within my heart"* (Psalm 40:7-8).

When He finds such, He equips and commissions into the field of His harvest.

Consecration

Consecration talks of being set apart for the Lord. It therefore implies a total separation from all that contaminates.

The first step of consecration is to give your heart to the Lord. All what happens to a man is determined by his heart's condition. That is why the Lord demands the heart of his children. Those who have given over their hearts to the Lord can joyfully live the consecrated life because they have their desires originating and being fulfilled in Him: *"My son, give me your heart and let your eyes keep to my ways"* (Proverbs 23:26) is a passionate request from the heart of our heavenly Father. Those who respond to this request from the Father have their heart in a safe place and the things which spring forth from the heart will only lead you along the path of righteousness so that you will ultimately fulfill your destiny.

The second step of consecration is to offer your body to the Lord.

"Therefore, I urge you, brothers, in view of God's mercy, to offer your bodies as living sacrifices, holy and pleasing to God--this is your spiritual act of worship" (Romans 12:1).

How do you offer your body as a living sacrifice? Just in the same way you offered your life to Him. When you cease to offer the parts of your body to sin and actively offer them as instruments of righteousness, then you are offering your body as a living sacrifice, acceptable and pleasing to God (Romans 6:13).

Surrendering

By surrendering, I mean abandonment into the hands of the Lord. It is living in the place where your every breathe is *"not my will but Yours be done"*. It is the unconditional willingness of the heart to do even that which brings pain and disrepute as long as it is in accordance with the will of the Master. It is a place where no disagreement with the will of the Father is allowed to last longer than a breath.

Do you remember the Master, in that eve of His crucifixion? The Bible says, *"'Abba, Father,' he said, 'everything is possible for you. Take this cup from me. Yet not what I will, but what you will'"* (Mark 14:36). That is the place where a surrendered person is. In fact a surrendered person is in some way vulnerable for he seeks not to defend himself because he shrinks back from nothing that would enhance the fulfillment of God's will in his life: *"Jesus commanded Peter, 'Put your sword away! Shall I not drink the cup the Father has given me?'"* (John 18:11)

These two verses portray the fact that David lived in this position of total surrender to the Lord:

"But now that he is dead, why should I fast? Can I bring him back again? I will go to him, but he will not return to me."
(2 Samuel 12:23)

"But if he says, 'I am not pleased with you,' then I am ready; let him do to me whatever seems good to him." (2 Samuel 15:26)

What about the incident with Shimei the rebel? David said, *"But the king said, 'What do you and I have in common, you sons of Zeruiah?' If he is cursing because the LORD said to him, 'Curse David,' who can ask, 'Why do you do this?'"* (2 Samuel 16:10).

David then said to Abishai and all his officials, *"My son, who is of my own flesh, is trying to take my life. How much more, then, this Benjamite! Leave him alone; let him curse, for the LORD has told him to. It may be that the LORD will see my distress and repay me with good for the cursing I am receiving today"* (2 Samuel 16:10-12).

If he was not in the place of absolute surrender he would allowed his men to deal with Shimei and free himself from the agony of the mockeries of this rebel. His decision to let the mockers mock is an act of surrendering.

Have you reached this place of absolute surrender? It is the best place for you because here the Lord takes charge of all that concerns you.

Conclusion

After all that has been said here, I want to let you know that growth can never be instant; it is a process. All the factors above must be carefully balanced for there to be proper growth and maturity in the life of an individual. Remember we said growth can be lopsided. Proper growth is a steady and healthy process. It is true that some people grow more rapidly than others, some become mature more readily than others. However, the ability to grow and become mature in whatever field lies within you and within your reach. Decide to, and be determined to attain maturity.

Other publications from the publisher

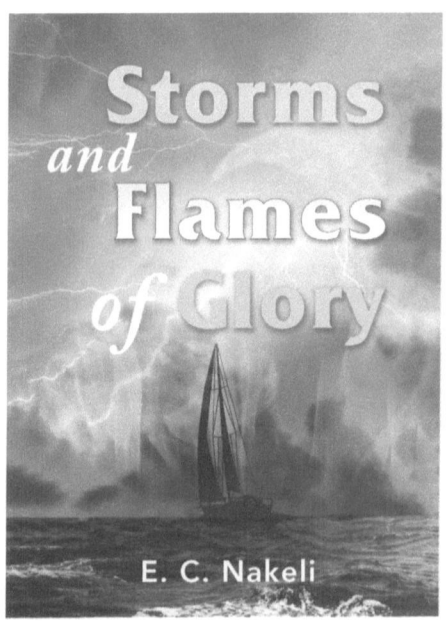

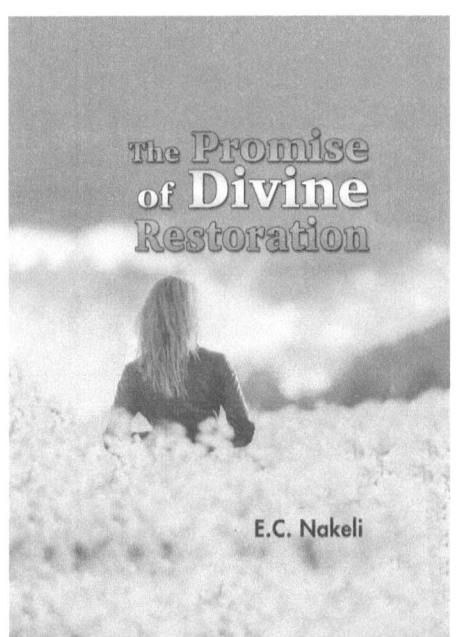

www.ingramcontent.com/pod-product-compliance
Lightning Source LLC
Chambersburg PA
CBHW020140130526
44591CB00030B/160